The **33**rd
an anthology

DREXEL
PUBLISHING GROUP

Editor	Gail Davida Rosen
Drexel Publishing Group Director	Scott Stein
Book Designer	Andrew Turner
Editorial Co-ops	Victoria Harrigan
	Henry Wood
Student Interns	Jordan Anderson
	Anna Bokarev
	Lucy Buchman
	Kasia Bunofsky
	Sanae Burrow-Burgess
	Akira Littles
	Maggie Patterson
	Anna Ramesh
	Aileen Ryan
	Béa Urbanowski-Womer
	Diamond Warney
	Randee Wismer
Faculty Proofreaders	Cassandra Hirsch
	Karen Nulton
	Donna Rondolone
	Fred Siegel
	Robert Watts

Sponsors

Drexel University
The College of Arts and Sciences at Drexel University
The Department of English and Philosophy at Drexel University

Dr. David S. Brown, Dean, College of Arts and Sciences, Drexel University
Dr. J. Roger Kurtz, Department Head, English and Philosophy,
Drexel University

The 33rd Volume 16
Drexel University
Department of English and Philosophy
3141 Chestnut Street
Philadelphia, PA 19104
drexelpublishing.com

Cover photo by Olivia Knestaut
Back Cover photo by Victoria Harrigan

The 33rd is published once a year.

Submissions are open in the spring, winter, and fall terms of each academic year. Manuscripts must be submitted as an e-mail attachment (MS Word). Visit drexelpublishing.com for submission guidelines.

ISBN 978-1-7324500-7-3

Deepest thanks to: Dr. David S. Brown; Dr. J. Roger Kurtz; all the judges from the Drexel Publishing Group Creative Writing Contest (Judith Curlee, Trisha Egbert, Valerie Fox, Cassandra Hirsch, Henry Israeli, Gregory Jewell, Lynn Levin, John Lynskey, Jill Moses, Matthew Mosher, Doreen Saar, Matthew Smith, Andrew Snover, Rebecca Spiegel, Nichole Stinson, and Errol Sull); the Drexel Publishing Group Essay Contest (Stacey Ake, Valerie Booth, Judith Curlee, Craig McClure, Erin Mccourt, Matthew Mosher, Karen Nulton, Margene Petersen, Marilyn Gaye Piety, Liz Polcha, Don Riggs, Donna Rondolone, Doreen Saar, Sheila Sandapen, Eric Schmutz, Fred Siegel, Maria Volynsky, Robert Watts, and Fengqing (Zoe) Zhang); the First-Year Writing Contest (Stacey Ake, William Albertson, Jan Armon, Valerie Booth, Trisha Egbert, Casey Hirsch, Liz Kimball, Roger Kurtz, Chris Nielson, Karen Nulton, Margene Peterson, Gail Davida Rosen, Doreen Saar, Sheila Sandapen, Fred Siegel, Matt Smith, Scott Stein, and Maria Volynsky); the Department of English and Philosophy, especially Liz Heenan; contest participants; and the Drexel Publishing Group staff.

17177 Laurel Park Drive
Suite 233
Livonia, MI 48152
800-562-2147
www.xanedu.com

Credits

Dettmer, Kathryn A. František Halas' "Whispered" and "Certitude" was originally translated and published in *Double Speak Magazine*, Spring 2022.

Fitts, Tim. "Flies" originally appeared in *Evening Street Review*, Summer 2022.

Hyatt, Jordan M. "A Pennsylvania Prison gets a Scandinavian-style Makeover—and Shows How the U.S. Penal System Could Become More Humane" (with co-author: Synøve Nygaard Andersen) was originally published in *The Conversation* on October 7, 2022.

Israeli, Henry. "Coattails" originally appeared in *Plume* Issue #135 in November 2022.

Kotzin, Miriam N. "Rosie Married Down" originally appeared in *Barely South Review*, Spring 2022.

Levin, Lynn. "The Silver Bullet" originally appeared in *Plume* Issue #116 on April 1, 2021.

McMillan Lecquie, Amanda. "'We Just like it Here'—Identity and Community in a Wisconsin Former Mining Town" originally appeared in *The Sociological Review* on December 6, 2022.

Mele, Leah. "Her Body Lines" originally appeared in *Philadelphia Stories* on July 21, 2022.

O'Connor, Keli B. "*Dans les Pas de Mon Père*" originally appeared in *The Spoonie Journal* on August 1, 2022.

Riggs, Don. "Review of *Cascade*" originally appeared in *The Future Fire Reviews* on December 22, 2022.

Snover, Andrew. "Water Ice Was the First One" was originally published in *Streetlight Magazine* Summer 2023.

Warnock, Scott. "The Rating is the Hardest Part" originally appeared in *When Falls the Coliseum* on December 19, 2022.

Zillmer, Eric A. "Why Music?" was presented at the XXIII Congress of the International Society of Rorschach and Projective Methods, in Geneva, Switzerland, as part of the *Inkblots and Music: The Rorschach Inkblot Concert* lecture in July of 2022.

Welcome

This edition of *The 33rd*, like all those that came before it, is one of the best expressions of the kind of liberal arts education on offer at Drexel. It is interdisciplinary, its range is wide, and it provides students with a wonderful place to practice and develop their craft.

While reading through these pages, one cannot help but feel pride in Drexel and all it does. It is a testament to the hard work of everyone who had a hand in producing this year's edition. This is my first edition of *The 33rd* as Dean and I am proud to be affiliated with such a dynamic group of faculty, staff, and students!

David S. Brown, Ph.D.
Dean, College of Arts and Sciences

Preface

You are holding the sixteenth annual volume of *The 33rd*, a unique anthology of outstanding writing by students and faculty from across Drexel University.

This book celebrates good writing, which means that it celebrates good thinking. We all know that writing is far more than just learning and following rules of correctness. Writing is actually our best tool for doing a university's basic job, which is to discover, preserve, and disseminate human knowledge. Writing is an inherent part of inquiry, of forging connections, and of communication. It is organized thinking.

Writing is especially indispensable at a place like Drexel University, where we pride ourselves on making our academic endeavors relevant to student success and to making our world a better place.

Cultivating curiosity and creativity in a supportive environment is a hallmark of our work in the Department of English and Philosophy. Whether it's through our MFA in fiction writing, through our community-based learning courses that connect with organizations and institutions in greater Philadelphia, through our many internships, or through other initiatives from the Drexel Publishing Group like *The 33rd*, our students find multiple outlets for their writing to reach the world.

All the essays and stories in this collection are adjudicated through a competitive review process. After publication, we use this volume as a textbook in many of our writing classes. The result is different every year, with new and creative surprises each time. What remains constant is the way that *The 33rd* embodies our mission of promoting imaginative and effective writing, starting right here on the street that gives the publication its name, and reaching out into a world that is limited only by our creative imagination.

Enjoy!

J. Roger Kurtz, Ph.D.
Professor and Department Head
Department of English and Philosophy

Table of Contents

First-Year Writing

Drexel Publishing Group Essays

Drexel Publishing Group Creative Writing

Literature Essay

Faculty Writing

Contributors

Writings Arranged by Context

Exploratory Writing

Fiction

Gender, Race, and Culture

Popular Culture

Science

First-Year Writing

Introduction

As Director of the First-Year Writing Program, I work with over 60 dedicated instructors who coach, cajole, and mentor 2,800-3,000 incoming students who produce tens of thousands of pages of writing. One of the best parts of my job is working with Jill Moses, our Assistant Director, on the First-Year Writing Contest.

This section of *The 33rd* includes essays written by the winners, runners-up, and honorable mentions from the contest that ran in the 2022-2023 academic year. Here is how essays get from our classes into this book:

- Students work very hard in their classes to produce lively, engaging writing about themselves and the world around them. Their instructors work hard, too, giving advice and encouragement throughout the writing process.

- Towards the end of the fall, we ask instructors to invite no more than two students from each of their sections to submit their best work to the First-Year Writing Contest. Last year, we got 100 excellent entries.

- With the help of approximately 20 faculty members, we go through a two-step judging process. After much deliberation, the judges come up with a winner, a first runner-up, a second runner-up, and seven honorable mentions.

- On the most wonderful day of the spring term, the winners, runners-up, and honorable mentions are announced at the English Awards Ceremony, along with the winners of various other contests. Furthermore, our winners receive prizes supported by a very generous endowment from the Erika Guenther and Gertrud Daemmrich Memorial Prizes.

- Finally, the editors of *The 33rd* step in to get permissions, to edit, and to create the book you are holding.

So, here is *The 33rd*. Your instructors in the First-Year Writing Program will ask you to read essays that won prizes last year so you can discuss them, debate them, and learn from them.

Are you interested in writing? Will you be in this book next year? On behalf of the First-Year Writing Program, we cannot wait to read your work.

Fred Siegel, Ph.D.
Director of the First-Year Writing Program

Following the instructions in chapter 3 or 4 of the *Writing Guide With Handbook*, write a literacy narrative or a memoir. Approximate length 750-1000 words.

—Professor Matthew Mosher

Aviv Amdur
My First Language

Is English my first language? Yes...but also, no?

For those of us who grew up in a bilingual household, the concept of a first language gets a little tricky. My mom, an immigrant from Israel who moved to the United States for her PhD, stayed here because she met my dad, who comes from a typical American upper middle-class family. So, when I think about what my first language is, the answer is both English and Hebrew. My mom filled my childhood with rapid-fire Hebrew, reading me Hebrew books, talking to me in Hebrew, giving me Hebrew CDs to listen to. My dad, on the other hand, spoke only in gentle English, as did my teachers, my babysitters, and my friends. I became the product of two different languages, two different cultures, creating odd amalgamations that were too English for Hebrew speakers and too Hebrew for English speakers.

"I'm cliffing," I would proclaim when my skin peeled after a sunburn (an odd combination of the Hebrew verb *lekalef* meaning "to peel" and English verb conjugation). I loved my "*Shisha*," (an approximation of the Hebrew word *smicha* meaning blanket). The invention of new Hebrew/English words was not uncommon in my household, to the point where my American grandfather gifted me a CD of patriotic American songs because he feared I was becoming too Israeli. That was my childhood, being pulled back and forth between my Israeli and American heritage.

Once I started going to school, my Israeli heritage began to slowly recede into the background. After all, it was English letters I was learning and English songs I was singing, and the Hebrew bubble I was used to while spending my days at home speaking with my mom burst. The American school system, intent on shoving as much "good English" down my throat as possible, left little room for "good Hebrew" improvement. With each year of school, I shifted further and further away from the Hebrew-speaking toddler I once was.

I retained my ability to understand spoken Hebrew. Hebrew is a fast, almost harsh language, with native speakers going a mile a minute, the words blending into each other until they can become an unintelligible sound mush if one isn't paying close enough attention. The Hebrew taught in synagogues and classrooms prepares students for the carefully pronounced and slowly spoken variety rarely found out in the wild. But I was lucky. That rapid native Israeli dialogue, full of slang and jokes and personality, that was my Hebrew. What I lacked was the grammar, the non-conversational words, and the ability to read and write.

We used to visit Israel for a month every summer, and I always looked forward to returning to the country that felt more like a second home to me than a vacation getaway. But looking at Hebrew on signs around me, their geometric shapes were foreign. I knew that if someone were to read them to me, my brain would conjure up meaning, concepts for what those sounds represented. But I hated having to be dependent on someone to read them out. Despite learning them at the same time, my English was now so far ahead of my Hebrew that the connection to my own family, my heritage, my culture was weak, I felt guilty calling myself Israeli. I would hear my mom and her family talking to each other, their words lively and spirited, the conversation ping-ponging from one person to the next in rapid succession as each person butted in to make a joke or give their two cents. How I longed to join in. But I couldn't, not without fear of butchering the verb conjugations that I was never taught, not without struggling to pull words out of the one-way wall that guarded the Hebrew in my brain. Their words went in, I'd laugh at the puns, at the funny stories they would tell, but I couldn't make any comebacks, I couldn't make any jokes of my own. I could only sit at the outskirts of the conversation and pretend to be a part of it, when I was only an observer.

It took me until high school to ask for help. I couldn't take a Hebrew class—partly because my school didn't offer one—but also because I was advanced in some respects and inept at others. I can know if something *sounds* wrong, I just don't have the ability to fix it. My mom reached out to an Israeli friend who used to be a Hebrew teacher at a university, and she agreed to tutor me. My Hebrew tutor was a motherly woman with a loud voice and an Israeli accent that brought me back to the streets of Tel Aviv. On the first day, she was impressed with my Hebrew comprehension, and pulled out a game box. "We'll start off small. I will shuffle the tiles and draw one. You just need to tell me a Hebrew word that starts with the same letter," she explained. My cheeks immediately reddened. "I don't even know what sound the letters make," I confessed.

Many Americans are young when they first learn to read. They forget the struggle of having to sound each letter out so slowly and carefully that they have forgotten the word by the time they reach the end of it. They forget how frustrating it is to look at a word and only see symbols staring back at them. They forget how you can entirely forget what sound a letter makes because it has not been in any of the words you have read recently. But I have not.

Each page we read together was grueling. I was transported back to kindergarten when my reading teacher would make me read a word over and over until I got it right. But I was not just doing this to have another language under my belt. I wasn't just doing this out of fascination for a place on my bucket list. I was doing this for my family, to be able to read what they wrote to me. For my mom, who came to a foreign country and made a life for herself. For myself, to not feel so lost in my own mind.

Each week, my tutor and I would meet. I'd read, conjugate verbs, and learn new words. Slowly, I moved on from children's books to magazine articles; vague characters became sounds which strung together to become words. Granted, it was still slow going. It took me minutes to read a sentence instead of seconds. But the fact I could read it at all gave me hope. When we went to visit my family in Israel, I got to use my new skills. I read anything and everything: signs, menus, labels, and billboards, occasionally asking, "Hey mom, what is this word?" Finally having the ability to understand the symbols felt like gaining access to an elite club, gaining access to a special part of my own family history. When my birthday rolled around, I was able to read the *"Yom huledet sameach hamuda!"* sent to me by my aunt and other well wishes from family and friends.

That simple act of reading the words by myself, that was the joy, the connection I was searching for. So, the answer is yes, English is my first language. It is the language I first learned to read and write in, the language I first wrote an essay in, the language I can most complexly express my thoughts in. But it is not my only first language. Hebrew is the first language I heard stories and songs in, the first language I said prayers on holidays in, the first language I felt a connection to. I don't have to choose one or the other. I am a combination of all my firsts, unable to be simplified down to a single language, a single culture, or a single identity.

Write a memoir/literacy narrative.

—Dr. John Lynskey

Kiana Ahmari

Farsi Class

Growing up, my parents taught me to stay quiet about my birth country Iran. Whenever someone asked me where I was from, I told them "Persia" and left them to wonder where it was.

Iran was—and still is—a very problematic country, both economically and politically. These problems have defined Iran since the Islamic Revolution, and it has made the country and the region a hotspot of domestic and international conflict. Because of this, I understood why my parents wanted me to stay quiet about Iran. The more I talked about it, the more questions I would get asked. I didn't—or shouldn't—have wanted that.

The only place I could comfortably share my Iranian identity with others was at gatherings. Persian gatherings were sort of like house parties—they encapsulate the wild energy of a house party, but without the crowds. These get together events were a way for my family to catch up with our Iranian friends, all while eating Persian food, drinking tea, and having fun.

Being surrounded by a group of Iranians had its struggles too. My primary struggle was what I call the "accent barrier."

I never lived in Iran, so I never learned to read, write, and speak there. Instead, I had to learn some of these skills in a small apartment 5,000+ miles away from Iran, with my parents as my teachers. My parents, knowing very well that we would never go back to Iran, let me learn and speak Persian in my own unique and "easy" way, hence, my accent consisted of a mix of the local dialect in Kerman (the Iranian province my parents grew up in) along with some English-ification of my sentence structures. Take the following Persian sentences:

Piano bâzi mikoni? (Do you play the piano?)

In Farsi, some words one would traditionally use in English do not mean the same thing in Persian. For instance, 'to play' the piano does not mean 'to play' the piano. Rather, you would need to say 'to hit' *(mizani)* the piano for it to mean 'to play' the piano. I make this error all the time. I tend to use the literal translation of a Persian word into my sentences, which can cause some issues when I try to speak with a fellow Iranian who has not been as exposed to English words as I have.

Ketâbeh beh dorhtaroo midi? (Will you give this book to that girl?)

The Kermani dialect uses vowels that aren't often seen in the Farsi alphabet. That's why we might randomly add the sound "-oo" (pronounced "*ou*") at the end of some words. Many Iranians find this dialect strange and funny, but I see it as a cute and unique twist to the language. Unless you are a fellow Kermani, the use of these vowels might throw you off and confuse you even further.

I knew very well that my accent was not seen as the "proper" way of speaking Farsi which is why I set out to learn how to read and write in Farsi. I hoped that in doing this I would get a better understanding of how Farsi is normally spoken in Iran.

My Farsi-learning journey started in a quiet and bland library classroom. My mom enrolled me in a local class taught by a former Farsi teacher, who like many Iranians during this day and time, had moved to America for a change in scenery and atmosphere. I was the oldest in the class, but age didn't matter to me. We were all trying to learn a language we were somewhat familiar with thanks to our parents. A month into the class, I had learned three new letters from the alphabet: *alef, ba*, and *noon*. I could make a few new words too, like *ab* (water), *baba* (dad), *nan* (bread), and the list goes on.

Learning to read and write in a language you have very little familiarity with other than what you learn of it at home is an interesting experience. It's like learning music, where you've listened to songs before, but as you learn about the different notes and signs used in musical composition, you get a better understanding of music theory and start writing your own music. As my knowledge of the different letters and symbols of the Persian alphabet grew, I wanted to do more with it.

I would show up to class some days, having completed two weeks worth of lessons. When my teacher saw how ahead I was from the rest of the class, she didn't approve of it.

"See students, when you read ahead in the book, you won't be learning as much in class. When I ask you to do the homework, only do the homework I assign you for this week."

I learned to never do that again.

To make the pace of the class manageable for the younger students, my teacher taught us at a very slow pace. Every two weeks, we would only cover one letter in class. Our homework mainly consisted of writing and rewriting the same words we had learned in class. Because of this, I found myself limited in what I could do with my newfound knowledge of Farsi. I couldn't write full sentences because I hadn't learned Farsi grammar yet. I couldn't read Persian books because I still didn't know how to read words without the additional short vowel marks on them. The speed at which I was learning Persian literacy felt slow.

While I struggled to stick to the pace of my Persian class, the people of Iran struggled to protect their right to freedom. As more Iranians tried to practice their basic human rights, the government would arrest them. Somedays, when I walked into the living room, I would see my parents scrolling through VOA and talking about the stories of people getting arrested in Iran.

"*Negâkon*, they arrested another young woman for not wearing her *roosari* [veil]."

"*Ey vây*, there's really no freedom whenever the *mullahs* are in charge. Remember that group of students who sang 'Happy' a few years ago? Something as simple as that got them imprisoned!"

"Have you talked to *hajj khanom* recently about what's going on with our family over there? It might be worth visiting them soon."

"You know it's not safe to travel to Iran, they could have us arrested and imprisoned for being 'foreign spies,' just like they did with those tourists last week."

These stories didn't make me feel any better about Iran, but they did make me curious about the politics, history, and culture of the country. How did such a government come to be in Iran? What was Iran like before the revolution? What sorts of influences have changed Iranian culture over the past century? And most importantly, what does Iranian television and literature say about the country?

I know my old Persian class wasn't going to cut it, so I decided to find another one to attend—one that was more 'my pace'. It didn't take long to find a Persian class that was close in proximity to Drexel. This class was what some call a "heritage" class—a literacy class for students of a certain linguistic background who only know how to speak the language. Looking at the syllabus for the course, I pictured myself in the class learning amongst other Persian "heritage" speakers. The best part about the course was the pace—it was a college course in that we would meet twice a week and be assigned homework.

I was not disappointed when I began taking the class. A week flies past and I had already learned and reviewed 6 letters in the alphabet—twice as many letters as I had learned in a month at my old class. Along with that, I had finally understood some of the differences between what we call spoken Farsi and written Farsi. I could also read Farsi passages and texts semi-fluently. Seeing this progress made me happy and reassured me that I could do more with the Iranian language. Not only can I speak and understand my Iranian family and friends, but I can read Farsi news articles about the issues Iranian people are facing.

With the most recent events going on in Iran, knowing both English and Farsi is very important in sharing Iranian's voice abroad. On October 1st, 2022, a few weeks following the killing of Mahsa Amini by Iran's Morality Police, I stood alongside fellow Iranian Americans in City Hall protesting against the oppressive rules of the Iranian Government. Together, we chant the words "زن، زندگی، آزادی" (*zân, zendegi, âzadi*), "woman, life, freedom." These three simple words mean a lot to the many Iranian people whose lives have been affected by the government in one way or another. These words also mark a call for change, from the Iranian community and the international community. As an Iranian living abroad, it is important for me to utilize my speaking and writing skills to spread this message.

Choose between writing a memoir or a literacy narrative.

—Professor Andrew Snover

Samya Bandukda
Titles and Trims

Snip, snip, snip.

Bits of my brown locks fell gently, almost gracefully onto the salon floor.

While most young girls grew up with their mums holding their hands through their first haircuts, I grew up with my mum holding the scissors. I pushed back in my swiveling salon chair, briskly dusting the fallen strands off my eyes to get a glimpse of the grand reveal. This was my childhood.

Along with other norms in Pakistan, gendered occupations were clearly defined. My father was a business-owner and my grandfather, a lawyer. It was a norm in my culture for my mother to be working in salons, cutting and styling hair. To me, *Amma* was an artist, using me as her blank canvas to experiment every style, dye and product in her palette. Our biannual ritual became one of cardamom tea and conversation as she snipped away at my untouched locks.

When I turned thirteen, my mum beamingly showed me a picture of a model with a crisp bob and neatly set fringe. Excitedly, I requested *"Amma, can I please have this haircut?"* Together, my mum and I traded my unruly mane for a mature bob, and, like that, my mum and I were tethered together with every trim.

At school, I reconnected with my friends, draped under the shade of a mango tree as we reminisced over the past school year and mapped out the one to come. *"Where did you get that haircut?"* one of them inquired. With confidence I replied, *"My mum did it."* As their smiles turned to glares, covered mouths and mocking brows, I couldn't quite understand their disdain. I promptly unfastened my *Dupatta* that was pinned across my chest, instead wrapping the fabric over my head to conceal *Amma's* creation.

Returning home from school that day, I glanced out of my car window, observing the desolate, timeworn streets of *Old Saddar Town*. Crumbling red-brick buildings, vacant carts once attended to by fruit vendors and antique dealers, unoccupied Cathedrals, all serving as souvenirs to grieve our independence from British rule. Although they left my country 75 years ago, the British had already sowed seeds of stratification and intolerance that would grow to linger in every facet of my life. I thought about how street signs still honored the names of English generals and veterans, how *Nani* (my maternal grandmother) no longer visits church in fear of another targeted shooting, how the young boy who waters our garden should be studying geography and history rather than thistles and orchids. I now noticed what it meant to be a victim of the splinters colonialism had left behind in Pakistan.

I realized firsthand that salon work was perceived as a trade of lower social classes. A divide to which I had remained oblivious became all the more real when my friends became ashamed of being in my company. I was granted the label, "*salon wali ki bachi*," the daughter of a salon girl. With a tainted perception of myself, I began letting my split ended hair grow wild, taking the long route home from school to avoid passing by *Amma's* salon. My favorite tradition with my mum slowly faded, and with it, our relationship decayed into one of shame and resentment.

Snip, snip, snip.

Bits of my grandmother's gray locks fell swiftly, rapidly onto the bathroom floor.

Her eyes glistened as tears gathered at the bottom of her aged lids, but for the sake of my presence in the room she did not allow them to fall. *Amma* no longer held her usual pair of scissors, instead, newly purchased ones. *Nani* had requested the shortest possible bob, a race against time before chemotherapy eventually beat her to it. As I observed my grandmother running her fingers through her newly clipped mane, I noticed how she never allowed her illness nor her label to define her. Around me, I realized that the women in my family each held their own respective title. My Nani, *an outcast*, a Christian married to a Muslim living in an Islamic, post-colonial republic. My cousin, *a divorcee*, carrying years of guilt imposed upon her by our conservative family. And my mother, the *salon wali* (salon girl).

All three were tainted by society's stereotypes, but I saw courage in each one of them. I took my usual route home from school the next day, observing Amma as she smiled and accepted a meager tip from a client. Turning back, she looked at me, pulling a funny face, sticking her tongue out and rolling her eyes. She wore her label like a badge of honor, owning society's perception of her, rather than granting it the privilege of owning her.

With the revived camaraderie my mum and I shared, I asked her to teach me her trade. The salon scissors, now in my hands, I learnt to accept the title placed upon me by my school peers. I recognized how she never let the shackles of tradition bind her, and the same way, no longer would I.

I still cut my own hair. Every new style, I flaunt, letting my hair flow freely and unforgivingly. Every new label, I embrace, owning their connotations confidently and unequivocally. As I stand at a crossroads of cultures, the intersection of my past and future selves, my mother's resilience serves as a mile marker to navigate the road ahead. When yet another of my new friends asks me who cuts my hair, I reflect on this winding, ever-unfolding journey: one of titles and trims.

Nani's Haircut, 1 February, 2017, Karachi Pakistan.

For this assignment, you may choose to write in either of two genres: literacy narrative or memoir

—Dr. Christopher Nielson

Julian Pittaoulis
A True Fish Story

On a typical Sunday afternoon, as I was finishing my early shift in a local fish factory, I was unexpectedly summoned over the loud intercom: "Julian Pittaoulis 6437, please report to the kitchen at the front. I repeat, please report to the kitchen at the front. Thank you."

I thought to myself, "Did I forget to complete something?"

I was exhausted and sore. My toes ached, and I was still shivering from the cold. Like most weekend days, I'd been working on the hectic shipping dock, loading trucks of squid orders and icing heavy boxes of Jail Island whole salmon filets with protruding pin bones since five in the morning. I was also in charge of making sure those orders were organized by route and alphabetical order, looking up at the big projector screen and matching cards to tags labeled by state. Lifting a skid of 100 pounds of Chinese Loligo for the Tropicana on Route J38 in Atlantic City and another 30 pounds of skin off bream for Barclay Prime on Route P15 in Rittenhouse Square was no easy task. I was barely able to lift my arms. I could not ever seem to catch a break or even receive an ounce of recognition. My manager briefly acknowledged my hard work stacking the Blu jumbo lump crab meat in the negative 10-degree freezer the week prior, but appreciation seemed rare in the distribution center, although it had taken diligent labor to learn the jargon of the shipping dock and, more importantly, the names and processes of preparing practically every variety of seafood in existence.

The wholesale seafood operation is mechanically complex, operating like the finest Swiss watch. Hundreds of aisles of fish stock sourced from all over the world are shipped, processed, packaged, and delivered daily. I am one out of hundreds of employees from diverse backgrounds working in synchronicity towards one common goal—to distribute fresh fish to the continental U.S.A. However, I often felt intimidated as a 16-year-old among the more mature, skilled workers.

I wondered what awaited me in the kitchen. I walked through the cutting room past shellfish alley, splashing in puddles of fluke head juice draining ever so slowly all over the floor from a ripped cardboard box, trying not to slip wearing my gigantic black boots three sizes too big. Buckets of salty seaweed were dumped over containers of Maine lobsters while buckets of cod were gutted and chunked by expert Vietnamese cutters. I passed by two employees talking about the Eagles playing the Vikings while filling up a tub so they could slack out the frozen octopus from Spain and wishing they could finish in time to watch the game. I threw off my reeking smock drenched in slime, scanned my badge to clock out, looked in a small mirror to try to smooth my unkempt hair, and emitted a tired sigh as I opened the door and wandered in still wearing my oversized work boots.

To my surprise, I was met with the music of "Summertime" by Ella Fitzgerald and Louis Armstrong from *Porgy and Bess*. An aroma of fine cuisine filled the room. Among the tables in the adjacent dining area was a decorative centerpiece of clams casino and tuna meatballs on a silver tray. Meanwhile, a group of finely dressed sales representatives were feasting around another table as they conversed and sipped wine from chilled coupé glasses. I felt out of place and confused. My expertise lay in the practical literacy of fish mongering and dock working, not the etiquette of rubbing elbows with executives, nor the manners of refined dining. But I was quickly greeted by a woman in a chef's coat and a man in a suit with an Oishi Shrimp tie. The Head of Sales, whom I had never met before, came towards me and enthusiastically introduced himself. Afterwards, he said, "Julian, I'd like you to meet one of the Executive Chefs at the White House. You have been quite the knowledgeable worker in the warehouse, and we thank you for embodying the characteristics of an ideal employee at such a young age."

The Chef jubilantly exclaimed, "What you are doing is extremely impressive; keep all those qualities with you as you continue to grow. I want you to have these cufflinks. They are from the Oval Office!"

I was shocked and speechless. I opened the petite black box labelled "Presidential." The gold metal pins with the shiny red, white, and blue flag mesmerized me. I shook hands with a tight and awkward grip. I could not believe what was happening. The Chef welcomed me to join the banquet, and I immediately dug deep into a meatball. After a delicious repast and an intriguing chat with the impressive culinarian, I sat in awe in the corner of the room, taking it all in.

This job turned into an expansive experience. I learned from my peers and managers the importance of honoring everyone's contribution to an important industry. Before I began my job at the wholesaler, I knew as much about seafood as anyone who merely ordered Filet-O-Fish sandwiches from McDonald's or scarfed down fish sticks at the high school cafeteria. But now, I was a bona-fide literate fishmonger who worked in collaboration with others to achieve a common goal. That day I realized what everyone had told me all along was true: rewards come from diligence and hard work. Just so I don't forget, I glance at my cufflinks everyday as a reminder.

For this assignment, you may choose to write in either of two genres: literacy narrative or memoir.

—Professor Gregory Jewell

Melissa Stellenwerf
A Timely Tradition

There's something about the smell of pungent vinegar dye early in the morning that marks the beginning of spring for my family. The air is crisp and cool not with the smell of snow, but of the smell of pollen and freshly picked tulips from my mother's front garden. After months of looking at the inside walls of my house, coming up with more new activities to fight off the winter boredom, my windows are finally open and the gentle morning sunlight illuminates the glass cabinet where we display our finished products. Every year they take us hours, from prep, to the actual decorating, to clean-up. Easter Day is always busy for my mother, Grandmother, and especially me. Although the process is straining and leaves my fingers sore and my eyes strained, there is nothing more rewarding than finally getting to melt the wax off my egg to reveal the intricate design left behind. The family tradition of decorating Ukrainian Pysanky Easter Eggs dates back to my grandmother's childhood and is still an incredibly important part of all of our lives today. Not only does this tradition strengthen the bond between my family members, but participating in an art practice from my cultural history further inspires me and my love for the arts.

After a restless night of sleep, our mornings start off early. I know it's time to start my day when I can feel the scent of the dye tickle my nose. Every year one dye stands out in particular. This year it smells like emerald green has taken the lead. My mother has already cleared the kitchen table and laid down the protective mat to shield our wooden table. Somehow this part of the schedule is new; my father figured we should give the table a break after years of wax battle scars and egg dye tattoos. Although the weather is starting to warm up, I can still feel the cold tile on my bare feet and see little dew drops balance on the spring green blades of grass in our back yard. The wooded regions of my back yard hide little portions of mulch still frozen; I can hear the satisfying crunches from my back door as my sister jumps up and down as if she were on a trampoline.

"Allie Belle come inside, we seriously need your help this year. And no, take off your sneakers before you come inside. Mom literally just swept up twenty minutes ago." My voice echoes through our kitchen and living room as I try to get my sister's attention.

My sister has never been too intensely interested in decorating Easter Eggs with the rest of us. My sister, father, uncle, and both of my cousins Zachary and Skyler opt for the more simple and mainstream method of design; the single dip. Every year without fail she chooses the brightest pink and leaves the egg in for hours, saturating it with the most vibrant shade of red imaginable. Sometimes my uncle will spice things up and dip his egg twice, once in blue and once in green. We mock him for being so detailed, after all, managing two colors is a lot to handle.

This year my mother has formulated even more colors. Thirty-seven if I counted correctly, everywhere from royal blue and spring green to monarch purple and canary yellow. The variety of options excites me, because it means more color combinations to experiment with. For the past week I've been scouring through Pinterest and Instagram, flipping endlessly through inspiration books my mother borrowed to find ideas for this year's final design. Although the actual finished egg never comes out as an exact replica of my sketch, having a rough idea of what I'm doing helps me focus and complete everything in one day. This past year has been difficult; the remnants of Covid-19 still spook my household, and the habit of staying inside is slowly being broken. This year my egg will display flowers, clear skies, patterns that will most definitely one-up last year's egg, and of course the family name.

Somehow, it's already 2pm and the cars start to fill my driveway. Soon enough my house is warm again with the vibrant smiles of my favorite people. Voices overlap with happy harmony and the feeling of pure joy rushes through my veins. That high-like sensation of seeing family members after long periods of separation gets us all ready and prepared to produce our best eggs yet. My grandmother sits at the front of the table. She hands me her long black leather jacket and smiles at me as she settles into her work area.

"She gets more and more beautiful every year, doesn't she Donna Jean?" my grandmother whispers.

"She does indeed." My mother's smile stretches across her face as she sits down in the chair next to mine.

She thinks I cannot hear her, but the smile I adopted from her shines even brighter as I collect the rest of my families' coats. All sixteen jackets pile up on my living room couches, and like clockwork, my cat jumps up to make himself comfortable. He'll be there all day, bathing in the soothing textures and midday sunlight. This year is special. I finally get to take my seat at the other long end of the decorating table. Usually, my mother and grandmother dominate the two head areas, but I've worked my way up the scale and my mastery had overridden my mother's. I feel proud and dominant sitting across from my grandmother as she has practiced her line-making for so many years. My grandmother's candle is lit, and we all can begin. My kistka is warm as I heat up the top portion and makes a clean, melty hole in the black beeswax I chose to work with this year. First up are all the sections I am choosing to keep white.

The process for coloring Pysanky eggs goes backwards. Each layer covered in wax preserves the color underneath. Because of this, lighter colors are used first such as yellows, light oranges, light greens and even sometimes reds, depending on the opacity of the dye. My first moves are strategic and careful as the hot wax flows out of the tip and onto the shell of my freshly cleaned egg. From here on out, my egg is my one and only priority. For hours I work creating little designs on the round surface, mapping out hidden gems and predicting color combinations that will both represent my own style of art and nod to the old-school palette of my elders. Soon enough the pale yellows, royal blues, and maroon reds will communicate while contrasting with the white shell to tell my own story. By 8pm our eggs are covered in wax entirely and it's time to reveal all our hard work. My mother brings over the jars of mineral spirits and we each submerge our eggs. I get a light pat on my back and a kiss on the cheek from my grandmother as I carefully carry her jar to our kitchen counter. While we wait our stomachs are rewarded with all types of Easter treats and beverages; the perfectly cooked ham tempts my tastebuds and they start sweating and aching to taste the savory meat. The room falls silent with light sounds of happy sighs while we feast together after a long day.

It's late but I can see my drawings peek through the dark thick covering. Carefully, I wipe away the excess wax and even more carefully empty my egg. As we stand together in a circle, admiring each other's finished products, I feel proud to be a part of such a talented and tradition-oriented family. My grandmother, mother and I sit our eggs next to each other in my mother's glass cabinet. Each egg's little throne is marked with jewels and glass. Another Easter day is done, but this wholesome tradition is far from over.

What is a question that you want to explore about deception and yourself?

—Dr. Karen Nulton

Alexandra Talarico
Cuore Della Famiglia—Misogyny in Italian-American Culture

Italians do this thing where we act like every goodbye is the last one we'll ever get. At 9 o'clock, my grandparents will decide that it's time to hit the road. They don't like driving much at night, and man, there's always traffic on the Verrazano Bridge even in the pitch black. Somewhere in our first round of goodbyes, someone will mention a story that will trigger a memory that will hold them up. A second cup of coffee will get poured for more biscotti to be dipped and we'll sync back into conversation, weary to let another interruption convince them it's time to go. "But really," they say after another hour, "we really have to be going, you've got school in the morning and the dark is no good for my eyes." We'll even stand up and get as far as the door until we realize we've forgotten to make plans for the next time we'll see each other. By the time it's finalized, we're on our third round of goodbye hugs, we have set plans for the next two months of weekend get-togethers, and it's starting to near 11 pm. They won't get home until a quarter after midnight, they may even hit traffic on the Verrazano, but even that's well worth it. I'm not quite sure if we hate goodbyes, or just like to linger before we go.

Italians do this other thing where we pretend that every hello is the first time we've seen each other in years. It doesn't matter if it's been two days or two months, we will always meet with a boisterous welcome and a too-tight hug. We linger then too, crowding the foyer, disappointed that our mouths can't move fast enough to tell each other what's changed since we've been apart and how much we've missed each other's company.

I don't remember which hour of hellos we were on when I realized how strange it was that my three brothers were always first asked about school while I was primarily interrogated on my love life.

Sometimes it feels like misogyny is just as much a part of Italian-American culture as our traditional "7 fishes" on Christmas Eve or our insistence to cook pasta *al dente*. For me, the remarks were never outwardly blatant. They were stuffed between the hugs, baked into ziti, and folded in our *mopeens*. While my siblings' futures were boiled down to their career prospects, mine was boiled down to becoming a mother. While their opinions were assertive and confident, mine leaned towards pushy and aggressive. While they were celebrated for their straight A's, I was toasted for helping my mom cook dinner. This was frustrating for several reasons, but mainly because 1) they know I've always preferred school over cooking and 2) I knew the slights weren't malicious. Grandparents, like everyone else, are a product of their generation. It's not their fault that their generation bred them to separate gender roles in the household and it's not their fault that they grew up in a culture where women were expected to uphold domestic tasks.

But that didn't matter to me. As soon as I realized what was happening, it became my mission to uproot their beliefs.

I decided that if I just got high enough grades, they would credit my academics and compliment my brain—and they did. After their, "but there's really *no* nice boys at school?" So then I decided to raise my bar. If I had ambitious enough career goals they would be more curious about my dreams than what shoes I was wearing. Again, they complied. They listened to me rave about science and medicine and the hospitals I dreamed of working at. After, of course, commenting that I should bake more because the cookies I had made were actually quite good.

I know that their comments weren't ill-hearted. They are interested in the boys I date because they're worried that I'm lonely. And they are fixated on certain ideals because they learned these beliefs from their parents who learned it from their parents who learned it from their parents. But even though I recognize this deep down, these separate gender roles that have been preprogrammed into my culture have been discouraging to me and millions of other young women. When you are constantly pressured into a corner that tells you your long term pursuits are not worth your time, it becomes easy to lean into the doubt and wonder if it's true.

In his article analyzing Italian-American literature, Chris Ruggerio comments on the "patriarchally defined" structure of Italian families noting that decades ago, girls as young as seven were "trained to take care for the household of her father which, in turn, serves as preparation for the care of her husband's household" (2). With these beliefs rooted in Italian immigrant culture, it's no wonder why my grandparents have certain expectations for who I'm supposed to be.

However, it's also important for me to note that my grandparents aren't only Italian, but New York Italian. My grandmothers, in particular, have a certain *charisma* in their bones that empowers them to mutter *"vafanapoli"* several times a day (*Vafanapoli* translates to 'go to Naples'. Or, for a more American twist, 'go to hell!'). My paternal grandmother wasn't *only* a mom or a wife, but a business owner and a successful one at that. She thinks it's funny that I've become "such a feminist" as I've gotten older, but I think it was inherent. I grew up with a mom who refused to marry her husband until she got her master's degree and a father who convinced me that I had the same capabilities as all three of my brothers (The latter was both encouraging and disastrous—I was just as capable as the three of them to play ice hockey, meaning I was equally as capable to take out the trash).

Still, around extended families, these microaggressions continue. And still, I couldn't stop them.

Sexism, unfortunately, isn't just an Italian phenomenon but is present in all cultures. However, the roots that started this misogyny vary. Ruggerio believes that the misogyny in Italian-American culture comes from this romanticized notion of an Italian woman that is often explored in male-dominated literature. In Italian families, the matriarch is 'revered', and often referred to as "the heart of the family" (2). Many male authors try to claim this role is powerful, perhaps just as powerful as the role working men have. While this sounds convincing, Ruggerio points out how "the fundamental distinctions in sex role socialization...subordinates the position of females" (7). In other words, women in Italian-American culture are *only* revered when they are wives and mothers, and this so-called "power" is only true in a domestic context. Because there is such a focus on the perfect Italian mother, straying from this mold and focusing on a career rather than a family is not only looked down upon, but considered shameful. Men can separate their identity from their families, but when women do the same, they "experience profound alienation" (5). And in a culture where you are taught from a very young age that family is everything, it's almost impossible to separate yourself from your family and maintain your identity.

Of course, as generations proceeded and the world entered into the 21st century, modern women became working women. Even for patriarchal Italian-Americans. When William Egelmen examined the working patterns of Italian American women in New York City during the early 2000's, he noted the shift that many women were making from the traditional matriarchal roles Italians idealized to a modern working woman. However, the old notions weren't dismissed as they began joining the workforce. Egelmen mentions a specific "cultural baggage" (188) that followed Italian women into work. Not only did they face the "challenges of the contemporary workplace" (195), but they also had to overcome the guilt that came from separating themselves from the cultural ideals they were taught since childhood.

If you're still not sold on the weight of this guilt, I'll propose this thought experiment: imagine an old Italian woman. I can nearly guarantee the woman you see is a gray-haired Nonna serving an eight course meal even though you already told her you ate before coming over. You would never imagine an entrepreneurial title agent (my grandmother) nor an anesthesiologist (my—fingers crossed—future profession). But if I ask you to picture an old Italian man (with no mob affiliation), you probably wouldn't be able to pin an image down. Italian-American women are expected to be wives and mothers and grandmothers, but no one expects Italian-American men to be husbands or fathers or grandfathers. When women don't meet these expectations, they feel like they are failing some unwritten cultural test. The question then becomes how can women separate themselves from this distinct cultural figure while balancing their ethnicity and femininity?

To answer this question, I sought the advice of one woman who has unknowingly shaped my distaste of the patriarchy: my grandmother. The daughter of Italian immigrants, Elizabeth Newell grew up embarrassed of her Italian parents and cultural identity. "While all of my friends had *normal* American dinners, we went to school not even knowing what french fries were," she tells me. Not only this, but with parents who didn't speak English, she shares how not knowing certain English words made her feel like an outcast.

While talking, she makes it clear that she "loves her family to death," but looking back there were certainly times when "things weren't how they were supposed to be." Unprompted, she shares how she hoped to go to college after graduating from high school, but her mother and older brothers simply wouldn't let her. "That's not what we do," she recalls her mother telling her. "Women don't work. We get married. We run the family." A chronic people-pleaser, she obeyed and married an Italian immigrant like the rest of her siblings.

This particular Italian is my paternal grandfather, and their relationship was a complicated one. "Women," she tells me, "were responsible for everything. Once you were married, you became the woman of the house." The repugnance in her voice as she says this mirrors the title "heart of the family" that Ruggerio mentioned in his article. "Women were expected to clean the house, make a menu, and prepare dinner. Men were expected to go out, make a living, come home, and do whatever they wanted. So when they sat down at the table, you were the one running around everywhere. If one of the kids were sick, you were the one taking care of them. It was really demeaning, I realize now."

We see these roles especially prevalent in pop culture. As Roseanne Quinn points out in her peer-reviewed 2004 article, pop culture has long misrepresented Italians as either "'dumb but lovable blue collar...characters'" or inherently a mobster, but particularly, the "misrepresentation [of Italian-descended women] has been pervasive, especially in terms of the multidimensionality of Italian American women's heritage, lives, and art" (par. 8-10). Quinn primarily discusses *The Sopranos*, an early 2000s series that focuses on mobsters and their personal lives. In *The Sopranos*, women do not exist on their own, but rather "in opposition to their male counterparts" (par. 13). Carmela Soprano, wife to protagonist Tony Soprano, is the definition of the 'perfect' Italian wife. Carmela is depicted as "metaphorically housebound" (par. 17) as she runs the household, preparing meals, agonizing over dinnerware, and constantly itching to be a picture-perfect host for her husband and her guests. In the beginning of the series, her character arc primarily revolves around "domestic issues," maintaining a household, and keeping Tony happy. However, as the show progresses, we see Carmela as a victim of not only domestic abuse but also "serial infidelity" (par. 16). Despite a brief separation, Carmela eventually reunites with Tony and falls back in line. Any regular mob-movie fan would recognize this as a popular trope for female characters—men cheat on, talk down to, and abuse their wives while the women are expected to keep their mouths shut—but any Italian would recognize that these gender roles aren't so far from the truth. Without the mafia backdrop and the soap-opera-style writing, these gender roles have been prevalent in Italian-American households for decades.

Unlike Carmela, my grandmother eventually left my grandfather. Also unlike Carmela, she got to make a name for herself outside of a male counterpart. "I became a partner in a title insurance company," she tells me. "And I was very proud of myself. I had a lot more control and I got to use all of the skills from high school that I wanted to after graduation. I think I did very well at it." She is now both happily retired and remarried.

When I ask her if she thinks those gender roles have shifted, she immediately says they have. "In the majority, I think things have changed for the better," she said. "Women who immigrated, who are now in their 70s and 80s have American born children, especially daughters, who say that's not right. This isn't how it should be. I don't want to be like you were. And this changed things."

While we spoke I realized for the first time the intensity of misogyny in my culture and the long line of women who have done their best to make a better world for their daughters and granddaughters. As much as I deceived myself into believing that I could change this deeply rooted misogyny, I also deceived myself into believing that in the decades since my family immigrated to America, nothing has changed. Both of these beliefs were untrue. Italian culture has long been built on the shoulders of mothers and *nonnas*, but I hadn't realized how Italian feminism has too. There is, of course, a long way to go until the romanticized notion of an Italian-American woman is washed away, there is proper female representation in pop culture, and the gender roles are completely dismantled, but there are also generations of women working to balance their ethnicity and femininity. This, I've realized, is present in my own family. Now, a granddaughter of Italian immigrants, I am encouraged to have a career and be a mother. I can be both an accomplished physician and a wife. I don't have to choose one or the other. This was propagated by my American-born parents and my American-born beliefs. Even if I face comments urging me in a certain direction, I know that I am free to forge my own path regardless of the cultural expectations I sometimes feel pressured to uphold.

Before we hung up, my grandmother and I lingered on the phone. She made sure I was adjusting well at school. I promised her I was. She asked how my new volunteer position at the Children's Hospital is going. I told her a story about a baby I held on Tuesday. We both can't believe Thanksgiving is so soon. She asked me if I was going to help my mom cook. Yes, I told her. I think this year I'm in charge of the apple pie.

References

Egelman, W. (2000). Traditional roles and modern work patterns of Italian American women in New York City. *Italian Americana*,18(2), 188-196. http://ezproxy2.library.drexel.edu/login?url=https://www.jstor.org/stable/29770040.

Quinn, R. (2004). Mothers, molls, and misogynists: resisting Italian American womanhood in *The Sopranos*. *The Journal of American Culture*, 27(2), 166-174. https://www.proquest.com/docview/918718096/abstract/17EF82DD98BC4142PQ/1?accountid=14572.

Ruggiero, C. (1986). Reclaiming the subject: Italian American women self-defined. *Explorations in Ethnic Studies*, 9(1).https://scholarscompass.vcu.edu/cgi/viewcontent.cgi?article=1312&context=ees.

For this assignment, you may choose to write in either of two genres: literacy narrative or memoir.

—Dr. Christopher Nielson

TJ Ton

Just Words on a Page

Everyone has felt the frustration that spawns from glaring at a devoid, white paper through strained eyes and an empty mind, and the dread of those precious seconds wasting away. We have all experienced that awful realization that what felt like only five minutes has become five hours. Whether in a gloomy school building or the comfort of my own home, when I am imprisoned within those four margins, time and reality become abstract. I am far too familiar with the grievances of looming essay deadlines, causing caffeinated days to fuse with sleepless nights as each moment pulls zero hours closer. In the hopes of not being alone, I would scour for someone like me and try to analyze the progress of my classmates. It would always bring me relief to hear, "I haven't started either."

Apart from those natural-born wordsmiths I envy in my dark hours of essay writing, I relished the fact that many people shared my aversion to writing assignments. The orchestra of harmonized moans and groans that followed the news of another essay brought a sense of community, and I believed that it was normal to hate the subject.

For as long as I can remember, I struggled with writing more than any other academic activity. Trying to pick through the chaotic chatter and crossfire of ideas in my head was like fishing for treasure in a garbage dump. Even when I had "good" ideas, I could not transcribe them. Brilliant and colorful visualizations in my head turned bleak and monochrome on paper. Scrawling out a simple cohesive sentence could take me forever, and I learned to despise English class, with my grades reflecting that.

I was repeatedly told, "You have too many meaningless sentences, cut them out" or "Your ideas are too unorganized, try to make them more concise."

As much as I tried to, I couldn't. My writing remained unstructured and overflowed with filler. As I was flooded with unrelenting streams of writing assignments, I could barely get by, and my essays reached a new level of rushed and "BS'd." This "flight or write" response, as I liked to call it, led to unhealthy amounts of procrastination bonded together with unproductive late-night writing sessions and all the stages of grief scattered along somewhere in between.

One day, I was given the assignment to interview a family member and author their story. Uninterested and unhappy, I prepared to trudge through this paper with two goals in mind: 1) get it done with as little effort as possible, and

2) keep my sanity intact. I decided to meet with my grandfather, and we began the interview.

"Okay. Could you please tell me your name and birthday?"

In the beginning, I just relayed generic questions and translated his answers into my notes. He was enthusiastic about talking, but I was less excited about the imminent writing portion that would follow.

"What was your job?" I went on.

"I was a soldier."

Although I knew my grandpa had been in the army, I had no other details. As we conversed, I was shocked to discover that he was a high-ranking lieutenant colonel in the Vietnam War. I took advantage of this moment to fulfill some of my curiosity, and I found us delving deeper into the topic of war. At this point, I was beginning to generate dozens of my own questions and was completely engaged.

"I still have a couple of metal souvenirs in my arm and leg," he remarked while grinning.

"What? How? Why are they still there?"

He guided my hand to his right arm and as I pressed my fingers down, I felt solid metal fragments along his thin skin. Next was his leg, where at the end of a long scar, I could feel the round tip of a bullet lodged in his calf. While rightfully shocking, to a teenage boy, this was also the coolest thing in the world.

"What else happened?" I blurted, a little too excitedly.

"I was captured." He paused.

After some contemplating, along with my begging him to share, he continued on to describe how he was a prisoner of war for almost 13 years. For each question he answered, I provided at least three more. At the end, I had pages of notes filled and felt pleasantly satisfied with my time with him.

Later that night, the familiar apprehensions began to resurface. It was time to write. As per usual, a good hour or two disappeared, and I had absolutely nothing to show for it. I didn't know how to start and felt stuck in place. I was losing motivation quickly and had to snap into it.

"Okay. It's time to get this over with. You can do it."

So of course, I sat for another hour or two, my keyboard untouched and my ideas nonexistent. Almost defeated, I flipped through my notebook, hoping to magically see an answer. As I read through my grandfather's experiences, they began to materialize in my mind and sort of come to life. I recalled the moments when he was sharing with me and began to wonder how it felt for him. Slowly, a daunting realization came over me: these are not just words, but instead are what he lived through. My grandfather had to endure those harsh conditions and terrible events for them to exist here in my notebook. Suddenly I could see him there, under the dense canopies of bamboo and vegetation. I could hear the gentle whisper of the forest, made up of distant animals and rivers. I could not, however, imagine the abrupt chaos and distress that ensued when the Viet Cong emerged from bushes and ambushed them. I could imagine the thundering explosions and pungent gunpowder and smoke clogging up the air, but could not imagine how it truly felt. The feeling of helplessness and terror as grenades fell from the sky and blasted flaming clouds of shrapnel in every direction was something he could never forget. I was overcome by emotions, imagining him crammed into a prison cell, injured and with nothing short of rags to shield him from nature's elements. I could never understand the pain he went through, counting every second of every day and praying it would be his last there, not knowing that 4,620 grueling days awaited him ahead. I wished we could preserve the overbearing joy he must have felt to be rescued and reunited with his family after more than a decade of horrors beyond my imagination.

That is when it dawned on me. There is a way to save these stories; ones that have only been told through fleeting words, dissipating into the air and never having the chance to be seen or cemented. By transcribing the interview, I was preserving my grandfather's experiences, and constructing his legacy.

It took me a long time to figure out why writing was invented in the first place and to determine if those ancient Sumerians were merely playing a cruel joke on us. However, on that day, writing brought me to a deeper understanding of something; that behind those words on a page, are stories. They are stories that develop from people's lives and years of experiences and emotions that are condensed so that others can experience them too. Literature preserves them in a way that merely speaking them doesn't. My eyes were opened to its true art and reading became so much more than just looking at an arrangement of symbols, it became listening to someone's journey. It became figuring out what led them to write and hearing about it straight from their soul. Memories deserve a home through writing, and to be shared and cherished. One of my favorite quotes, attributed to Ernest Hemingway, states, "There is nothing to writing. All you do is sit down at a typewriter and bleed." This quote is how I like to view writing now, because I don't wish to just mouth words; I want to bleed my trials, my tribulations and sufferings, my reality straight from my heart's core onto that page. And I have learned that's what good writing should be.

Evaluating and Solving Problem: For this assignment, you will research a problematic issue, propose one or more solutions to the problem, and present an argument supporting your solution. One effective way to approach this assignment is to identify a problem in a profession or discipline of interest to you. Another is to deal with a problem local to Drexel, Philadelphia or your hometown, and relevant to your experience there. The topic should be original and significant.

—Professor Bob Finegan

Justin Veloz
The Current State of Traumatic Brain Injuries in Mixed Martial Arts

In 2015, a young boxer named Prichard Colon stepped into the ring, like any other time, without any knowledge that it would be his last fight before his life would change. During his fight with Terrel Williams, Colon complained about pain at the back of his head, likely caused by illegal punches he sustained. During the seventh round is when ringside Dr. Richard Ashbly should have stopped the fight, but it continued until Colon was disqualified in the ninth round when his team removed his gloves, falsely thinking it was the final round. Shortly after the blunder, Colon was taken to the hospital "where emergency brain surgery evacuated a subdural hematoma and relieved pressure on his skull" (Weinbaum). The experience left him in a vegetative state. As time passes, Colon is still recovering, but only time will tell how far.

Traumatic brain injuries (TBI) are nothing to be taken lightly, as shown by Colon's life-altering injury. The most well-known example of TBI is a concussion. The CDC estimates that 5% of people experience some degree of TBI annually (Georges). In combat sports like MMA (Mixed Martial Arts), athletes compete against each other in grappling, striking, or mixed style discipline (Barley). A recent meta-analysis conducted by Dr. Lucas Lim from Singapore's Institute of Mental Health showed that in MMA, the "most commonly injured anatomic region was the head," making up between 68.8-78.0% of injuries, with concussions making up between 3.8-20%. In kickboxing, a study showed 19.2 concussions occurring for every 1000 fights (Neidecker). These large ranges of fighters believed to have suffered TBI demonstrate the larger issue; that doctors still cannot diagnose TBI with certainty due to limited observational tools and individuals showing no physical symptoms. To alleviate these issues, more research is needed to better diagnose and treat these injuries. Chief of Neurosurgery at Zuckerberg San Francisco General Hospital, Geoffrey Manley, states that accompanying this high rate of head injuries in combat sports are various conditions that exacerbate the problem, by increasing the likelihood of more life-altering cases of TBI that can cause anything from vomiting and headaches to paralysis and death.

Many elements play a role in the presence of brain injuries in combat sports, but weight cutting might be the biggest issue. Athletes are separated by weight to promote fairness, so fighters are weighed before fights to compete against an opponent of their size. On paper, this sounds reasonable, but as Edith University health and sports science professor Oliver Barley explains, because of how most weigh-ins are structured, athletes often "attempt to gain a competitive edge and be paired with a smaller opponent by losing significant body weight" through an extreme caloric deficit or dehydration. Dehydration typically entails not consuming fluids while utilizing saunas and sweat suits to drain the body of fluids, thus reducing mass. This practice stresses the brain by starving it of sufficient nutrients to function and "potentially increase[s] the risk of brain injury arising from head trauma" by removing the cerebrospinal fluid that cushions the brain (Barley). Combat athletes then rehydrate after weighing in, but research is unclear on whether full rehydration is possible within the 24 hours typical for them to fight after being weighed. The impact on athletic performance is unclear when valued against fighting smaller opponents, but the physically and mentally unhealthy practice remains prevalent (Barley).

The elevated risk of concussions associated with dehydration makes changing the culture of weight-cutting in combat sports a priority. To tackle this issue, fight promotions could introduce more weight classes offering the opportunity for fighters to compete at a comfortable weight (Barley). In MMA, most weight classes are separated by 10 lbs., in contrast to boxing and kickboxing being every 5 lbs. Implementing hydration tests paired with less time between weigh-ins could help deter fighters from cutting weight as they risk not being able to compete or rehydrate and thus attenuate occurrences (Barley).

Unlike traditional contact sports, inflicting damage on your opponent is the objective of combat sports. However, just because concussions are a possible outcome, it does not mean that athletic commissions can neglect to provide proficient procedures for treating concussions (Neidecker). Improving regulation applies to both ringside physicians' guidelines in identifying concussions and guidelines demonstrating a proper recovery process that reduces the likelihood of extensive damage. What is important to understand about concussions and TBI is that they are cumulative, whereas damage can build up, resulting in worse conditions like chronic traumatic encephalopathy (CTE) which stems from repeated concussions (Lim). CTE can only be identified postmortem.

Currently, concussion guidelines lack consistency. Some organizations only permit referees to stop a fight, while others extend the power to ringside doctors. According to sports medicine physician and President of the Association of Ringside Physicians John Neidecker, doctors should be allowed to stop fights, to ensure the prolonged health of competitors, as they can prevent further TBI from occurring. Additionally, there need to be clear guidelines for medical suspensions, where fighters' suspension time increases for consecutive knockouts and for athletes who lose consciousness for longer than an instant (Neidecker). Giving fighters the correct time to recover from concussions reduces the risk of further concussions.

It is difficult to discuss concussions in combat sports without the topic of headgear being mentioned. According to sports sociologist Anne Tjønndal at Norwegian University of Science and Technology, headgear use in combat sports primarily offers "protection against skull fractures and cuts to the face and ears" while the relationship with concussions is still unclear. Headgear can absorb some force from punches, but not enough to suggest competitive use. An overlooked danger of headgear is the loss of ability to accurately determine damage due to lack of visible injuries. Further evaluation shows that training is a hotbed for most injuries, therefore, headgear may have a place in training as it is less intense but more frequent and thus contributes to concussions (Tjønndal).

Traumatic head injuries will never be truly eliminated in combat sports. By implementing measures to reduce weight cutting, allowing doctors to intervene, and giving fighters the appropriate time to recover, the frequency and severity of TBI can be reduced (Barley; Neidecker). By addressing the cumulative nature of concussions, combat athletes could focus on improving their skills like any other athlete.

Works Cited

Barley, Oliver R et al. "The Current State of Weight-Cutting in Combat Sports-Weight-Cutting in Combat Sports." *Sports* (Basel, Switzerland) vol. 7,5 123. 21 May. 2019, doi:10.3390/sports7050123.

Georges A, M Das J. Traumatic Brain Injury. [Updated 2022 Jan 5]. In: StatPearls [Internet]. Treasure Island (FL): *StatPearls Publishing*; 2022 Jan-. Available from: https://www.ncbi.nlm.nih.gov/books/NBK459300.

Lim, Lucas J H et al. "Dangers of Mixed Martial Arts in the Development of Chronic Traumatic Encephalopathy." *International Journal of Environmental Research and Public Health* vol. 16,2 254. 17 Jan. 2019, doi:10.3390/ijerph16020254.

Manley, Geoffrey T., et al. "Concussion and Other Traumatic Brain Injuries." *Harrison's Principles of Internal Medicine*, 20e Eds. J. Larry Jameson, et al. McGraw Hill, 2018, https://accessmedicine-mhmedical-com.ezproxy2.library.drexel.edu/content.aspx?bookid=2129&sectionid=192533001.

Neidecker, John et al. "Concussion management in combat sports: consensus statement from the Association of Ringside Physicians." *British Journal of Sports Medicine* vol. 53,6 (2019): 328-333. Doi:10.1136/bjsports-2017-098799.

Tjønndal, Anne, et al. "Concussions, Cuts and Cracked Bones: A Systematic Literature Review on Protective Headgear and Head Injury Prevention in Olympic Boxing." *European Journal of Sport Science*, vol. 22, no. 3, 2021, pp. 447–459., https://doi.org/10.1080/17461391.2021.1872711.

Weinbaum, William. "Parents of Ex-Boxer Prichard Colon Seek More than $50 Million in Lawsuit." *ESPN, ESPN Internet Ventures*, 3 May 2017, https://www.espn.com/boxing/story/_/id/19301313/the-parents-former-boxer-prichard-colon-suing-ringside-doctor-promoters-more-50-million.

Write a researched composition about deception.

—Dr. Karen Nulton

Conway Zheng
Not a Coming Out Story

It was really sweet when I watched *Love, Simon* (2018) while being wrapped up in comfy blankets on a friend's couch. It was nice to see a positive representation of gay people in mainstream media without tragic endings arising from their sexuality and home lives. Instead of being rejected when our high school teenager, Simon, came out to his parents, they accepted him, embraced him, and apologized to him for how long he must have endured while hiding his sexuality. It was a bittersweet moment for me during that emotional scene because I was seeing a character living out a dream that I will never catch. The blankets around me soon felt like stuffy, prickly, constricting bandages as I imagined my own "Love, Conway" and my coming out story with my traditional Asian parents. And it is a disillusionment with what is represented in the media.

As a Chinese American who is a part of the LGBTQ+ community, I have to live two separate lives. When I am out with my friends, I am sassy, flamboyant, and expressive. I speak with a variety of pitches and intonations, like my voice is bursting out with my laughter. They all know my sexuality, and we share a sense of humor that I could not share with straight guys. But, with a swing of the front door and a change of language, I am no longer out, both literally and metaphorically. Parallel to my personality at home, my voice in Mandarin drops and becomes monotonous. My parents are homophobic, and I can never show them the gay side of my identity without facing backlash, shame, and possibly eviction from their home. And so, I am forced to juggle between my identities of being an Asian son and a gay man without colliding the two worlds together.

Unlike the Western society of including LGBTQ+ people in their media, Eastern countries often have no such representation. For China, the concept of homosexuality goes against many of the culture's values. A core foundation in forming the hierarchy and order within a Chinese family is the philosophy of filial piety brought on by Confucianism. Filial piety places supremacy upon one's elders and parents. Children are expected to have the utmost respect and obedience for the people that have birthed and raised them; they are "obligated to prioritize their parents before other duties" (Pei 2019). Within the Confucius ideology, there are three idioms that establish the context for modern-day Chinese parents' beliefs: "[If the family lives in harmony, all affairs will prosper]," "[Filial piety is the virtue of prime importance]," and "[There are three forms of unfilial conduct, the worst of which is to have no descendants]," (Zhang 2014). The first two phrases succinctly describe Chinese society's value of family, and the third phrase establishes a person's duty to pass down their family name and blood. In conjunction, China is a collectivist culture that emphasizes harmony among the group (family, neighbors, community, and society as a whole) over the freedom of individualism, which is valued by Western societies. Thus, Chinese culture "[devalues] those individuals who do not conform to group values because they are thought to damage social harmony" (Pei 2019). In just this context, LGBTQ+ Chinese people face immense pressure from both family and society to be "normal" and to perform their duties as sons and daughters of their parents.

Due to China's culture of filial piety, Confucianism, and collectivism, Chinese parents strongly value heterosexual marriage and the continuation of the family. As a result, homosexuality is heavily frowned upon and shamed by the community. In a national survey across 31 Chinese provinces, the "acceptance of having children who identify as LGBT" was the lowest for "heterosexual participants" despite them having higher tolerance for LGBTQ+ people in other contexts (Wang 2020). This further indicates the significance of marriage and legacy for Chinese people and how LGBTQ+ children would face rejection from their parents due to their inability to complete either of those two duties.

In the U.S., the importance of marriage or having grandchildren may differ between families, but almost every Chinese parent vocalizes their wishes for their children's marriage. I was only in elementary school, not even ten years old yet, when my parents were already engraining the ideals of filial piety and marriage in me. Many times, I had to hear the same speech from my mother: "You must get a good job in the future. You must also marry a smart and beautiful girl and buy a big house so we can all live together." At the same time, throughout my childhood, I had seen a decade of attempts from my parents to convince my bisexual older sister to find a husband. They consistently enjoined my sister to get married and have children. Beyond parental pressures, queer Chinese people must also deal with being "considered a form of shame for one's family," "[making] the family the subject of vicious gossip," and "[stigmatizing] the family name." In addition, "Parents of LGBT individuals will also be blamed for raising children who will fail to uphold their duty to carry on the family line" (Wang 2020). For gay Chinese men, the pressure to marry is not just from their parents. Due to their upbringing with filial piety and China's collectivistic culture, their individual actions affect not just themselves but also their family. Not only do they fear their parents' shame, disgust, and disappointment, but they also feel extreme guilt for causing such disgrace and burden to their family.

In an article, one Chinese man said "it was so hard to tell my parents... especially my dad. He loved me so much." And for another man, his, "parents demanded that their son find a girlfriend and bring her to social and family functions so that he would appear normal in front of all their relatives and friends" (Bie 2016). These societal and parental pressures and guilts are so strong to the point that many queer Chinese men will "marry heterosexual women" or "a lesbian so that they will appear to be a normal married couple" (Bie 2016). In the complete opposite manner to the coming out stories shared on social media in the U.S., these gay men go through extensive lengths to stay in the closet and to avoid disaster within their family.

My sister currently lives in another state with her girlfriend, whom she refers to as a friend or roommate whenever my parents bring her up. My sister was reluctant to talk about being part of the LGBTQ+ community, likely because she still shares similar views as my parents or prefers to keep such saddening or shameful topics unspoken. In my interview with her, I was only able to get a few answers out of her. When I asked if she would ever come out to our parents, she dismissively shut down the idea. She explained how, "your mom has nerve issues when she experiences strong emotions. Coming out to her would make her suffer from a stroke and kill her." And she even warns me not to come out either. My sister was born and raised in China and thus has a stronger connection with the culture than I do. She has never gone to any LGBTQ+ events nor participated in any online discussions about such issues either. She is already 33 years old and will continue to hide her sexuality from my parents for the rest of their lives. My sister also spoke about how a person's sexuality should not be other people's business and we should keep these topics to ourselves—continuing the idea of conformity and collectivism within the Chinese culture. Her lifestyle of keeping her personal life to herself and not troubling our parents is shared by many LGBTQ+ Chinese people.

But what about Asian Americans, who are more influenced by the Western ideas of individualism and the more lenient expectations of American society? Even so, they are still under the rule of their traditional Asian parents. An example of the parents' influence over their children is the extracurricular activities that their children are (or are not) involved in. Many Asian children pick up music lessons or disregard sports to focus on studying due to their parents highly valuing "the academic and musical pursuits of their children" (Pang 2015). Even common within Western LGBTQ+ movies and films are the protagonists' fears of their parents' expectations and beliefs. But for Asian Americans, their coming out stories often end in tragedy.

"'It gets better,' but for Asian Americans, coming out can also get complicated" is an article from *Voices*, a student program by the Asian American Journalists Association, which chronicles the coming out stories of several Asian Americans. The majority of the stories follow the same pattern of rejection from one's parents as experienced by LGBTQ+ Chinese people back in China. One Chinese American transwoman said, "Being the oldest son...I had a whole world of expectations on me, and by giving that up, it was like all their dreams kind of crashed." Another Vietnamese American explained, "My parents came from Vietnam, came from the war...they sacrificed a lot to be here," she said. "So I battle a lot with my identity [and] carry a lot of guilt [because] why do I have to make this harder for my parents, who wanted the good life, who wanted their kids to have a good life?" (Fischer-Hwang 2021). Although Asian Americans may not face the societal expectations demanded by their parents' native country, they now, as children of immigrants, face another dilemma. Our parents have worked tirelessly to secure a better life for us in the U.S. My parents have worked day and night over weekends and holidays in their Chinese restaurant for decades to secure a home and a better standard of living for me and my sister. For their sacrifices (and the importance of filial piety), I should be grateful to my parents and listen to their every wish. However, my very own identity as part of the LGBTQ+ community disrupts many of their wishes. Even though social media and friends have made me proud of being gay, I still feel ungrateful for being unable to repay my parents in certain ways. For Asian Americans, coming out is still a struggle to find the courage to overcome the harsh reactions of our parents. But in addition, we must also deal with our identities as children of immigrant parents, which often lead to feelings of guilt as we stray from our parents' wishes.

The messages and themes often portrayed by LGBTQ+ movies, social media, and members within the community here in the United States are acceptance, self-love, and not listening to what society tells you. However, this is only a glamorized fantasy for many queer Asians due to their traditional parents' heterosexism. Specifically in China, many LGBTQ+ members are brought up to respect their parents and to follow the social norms of forming a family. They are unwilling to come out due to the shame and stigmatization of homosexuality and are sometimes forced to marry the opposite-sex to hide their true identities. As for Asian Americans, due to their blend between the Western and Eastern cultures, they can express their pride, but only outside (U.S. peers) of their homes (Asian household). Simultaneously, as children of immigrant parents, who worked so hard for their futures, Asian Americans may also feel guilt for their sexuality and inability to fulfill the wishes of their parents. These emotions compound as further incentives to keep Asians and Asian Americans within the closet.

However, on a brighter note, some parents can learn and change their minds. For Le Tang, a Chinese-Vietnamese American lesbian, after months since her mother's initial, harsh reactions toward the daughter's coming out, Tang's mother had become accepting of her. Tang's mother had done research about being lesbian and concluded that Tang is still her daughter and would love her no matter what (Fischer-Hwang 2021). And in my conversations with my mother, I believe she already suspects my sister's relationship with her "friend" but she would not confront my sister because she is just fine knowing my sister would not be lonely in the future.

Works Cited

Bie, B. & Tang, L. (2016). Chinese gay men's coming out narratives: Connecting social relationship to co-cultural theory. *Journal of International and Intercultural Communication, 9*(4), 351–367. https://doi.org/10.1080/17513057.2016.1142602.

Fischer-Hwang, I., Takahashi, L., & Wu, G. (2021). "It gets better," but for Asian Americans, coming out can also get complicated. *AAJA Voices*. Retrieved from https://voices.aaja.org/index/2018/8/8/it-gets-better.

Pang, B., Macdonald, D., & Hay, P. (2015). 'Do I have a choice?' The influences of family values and investments on Chinese migrant young people's lifestyles and physical activity participation in Australia. *Sport, Education and Society, 20*(8), 1048–1064. https://doi-org.ezproxy2.library.drexel.edu/10.1080/13573322.2013.833504.

Pei, W. (2019). An Investigation in the Chinese LGBT People's Online Coming-Out Narratives: Cultural Influences, Co-cultural Practices, and Outcomes (Order No. 22618696). Available from ProQuest One Academic. (2306522889). Retrieved from http://ezproxy2.library.drexel.edu/login?url=https://www.proquest.com/dissertations-theses/investigation-chinese-lgbt-people-s-online-coming/docview/2306522889/se-2.

Wang, Y., Hu, Z., Peng, K., Rechdan, J., Yang, Y., Wu, L., Xin, Y., Lin, J., Duan, Z., Zhu, X., Feng, Y., Chen, S., Ou, J., & Chen, R. (2020). Mapping out a spectrum of the Chinese public's discrimination toward the LGBT community: Results from a national survey. *BMC Public Health, 20*(1), 1-10. https://doi.org/10.1186/s12889-020-08834-y.

Zhang, Q. F. (2014). Transgender representation by the people's daily since 1949. *Sexuality & Culture, 18*(1), 180-195. doi: https://doi.org/10.1007/s12119-013-9184-3.

Drexel Publishing Group

Essays

Introduction

The following essays were selected from student submissions to the Drexel Publishing Group Essay Contest. The contest was judged by faculty from a wide range of disciplines in the College of Arts and Sciences. This was a very competitive contest that required two rounds of judging. The essays in this section of *The 33rd* explore diverse topics such as education, culture, the environment, and literature. These student writers demonstrate their fine research skills in a variety of disciplines in the arts and sciences, and do so with originality, nuance, and passion.

To honor the stylistic requirements of each field, we have reproduced the essays in their original forms.

—The Editors

Kathleen R. Grillo
An Analysis, in Three Essays, of Sherlock Holmes' Society

Literature is inherently a reflection of its society. Authors, whether consciously or subconsciously, implant ideology of their current society within their stories. The mystery story does not stray from this, even if many of them follow the same format: some form of a crime, typically murder, has been committed and must be solved. This is a story arc that has been done for centuries and has not changed much in that time, but the characterization, settings, and even the crimes themselves, illustrate the essential aspects of the society in which they are written.

This concept is essential to the Sherlock Holmes stories, explained by Stephen Knight in his essay, "The Case of the Great Detective," Catherine Belsey in her essay, "Deconstruction of the Text: Sherlock Holmes," and Rosemary Hennessy and Rajeswari Mohan in their essay "The Speckled Band: The Construction of Women in a Popular Text of Empire." Each of these essays looks at the society of the Sherlock Holmes stories and their author, Sir Arthur Conan Doyle, to better understand the nuances of characters, setting, and plot. In addition, these essayists establish the relationship Victorian society had with the Sherlock Holmes stories.

Knight's essay, "The Case of the Great Detective," examines the popularity of the Holmes stories in their time. He asks the question "What then were the values that gave power to the Holmes phenomenon—what does the great detective stand for?" (Knight 368). Knight answers: science. He states that as science grew in importance to the Victorians, Doyle implemented this in his character of Sherlock Holmes. Doyle, Knight explains, was disappointed in the crime fiction of his day as it "depended on luck as the solution" (Knight 369). So, in his formation of Sherlock Holmes, he made sure the detective relied on the collection and analysis of evidence. Doyle was careful, though, in how he used science. Although the Victorians grew to enjoy science, they had an inherent fear in science that was anti-humane. To counteract this, Doyle characterized Holmes as an individual, another major ideology of the Victorians. Doyle humanized Sherlock with his character's eccentricities.

The second question Knight asked was not of the character of Sherlock Holmes, but the crimes of his stories, stating that the crimes committed reflected the society of Victorian England as much as the story's characters. Of the crimes he says, "Broadly speaking they deal with disorders in the respectable bourgeois family" (Knight 370). Knight explains that the crimes used in any mystery story exemplify the fears of its society. In Victorian England, the most feared crimes were those that disrupted bourgeois life. He uses "The Speckled Band" and "The Red-Headed League" as examples. In "The Speckled Band," a father kills his stepdaughter before her wedding in his greed to obtain her money. In "The Red-Headed League," a servant betrays his affluent employer to steal his family's treasure. As with many of the Holmes stories, these examples stem from what Knight says is "The fear that selfish greed could become disorder..." (Knight 372).

In Catherine Belsey's essay, "Deconstructing the Text: Sherlock Holmes," society once again is at the forefront of the conversation, taking a special analysis in the eyes of classic realism. Like Knight, she looks at the scientific method of Sherlock Holmes, but unlike Knight, Belsey takes an in depth look at the place of women in the Holmes stories and how their perception within those stories presents an inadequacy in Doyle's science. She begins by examining specific female characters within one of the Holmes stories, Lady Eva Blackwell and Milverton's housemaid from "Charles Augustus Milverton." In this story, women are used only as a plot device, rather than fully formed characters. Lady Blackwell herself only exists in the form of a letter sent to Sherlock to hire him and Milverton's housemaid, who is not even given a name herself, becomes Sherlock's fiancée, but only so she can provide him with information of Milverton's home. Even further, the murderer of the story, who was also being blackmailed by Milverton, is an unnamed and unidentified woman. Belsey points out her main conflict with Doyle's treatment of women within the Holmes stories, saying "The sexuality of these three shadowy women motivates the narrative and yet is barely present in it" (Belsey 383).

Belsey goes on to explain the explicitness of the Holmes stories. Much like Knight's argument for Doyle's use of the scientific method, Belsey describes Doyle's work to create a transparent realism within the Holmes stories. Sherlock's conclusions to the mysteries of his cases are based in deductive reasoning. The allure of these stories comes from their ability to so easily capture realistic issues of Victorian society. Yet, as Belsey points out,"...these stories, whose overt project is total explicitness, total verisimilitude in the interests of a plea for scientificity, are haunted by shadowy, mysterious and often silent women. Their silence repeatedly conceals their sexuality, investing it with a dark and magical quality which is beyond the reach of scientific knowledge" (Belsey 385). Thus, Belsey concludes that the science Doyle works so hard to implant into Sherlock Holmes and his mysteries is overshadowed by his lack of realism in his female characters.

"The Speckled Band: The Construction of Woman in a Popular Text of Empire" by Rosemary Hennessy and Rajeswari Mohan explores, like Knight and Belsey, the interaction between the Sherlock Holmes stories and Victorian society. Unlike Knight, and like Belsey, Hennessy and Mohan focus their essay's attention on the position of women in the Sherlock mysteries. The two authors take a specific look at the Victorian political world for women, in accordance with its effect on the women of the Sherlock stories. The authors point out their main criticisms of Doyle's writing, specifically in the form of Sherlock Holmes's character. They find that Doyle constructed Holmes as "rational protector, the resolution of the narrator's enigma, and the positioning of the reader."

They do this by taking a specific look at "The Speckled Band" as Knight mentioned in his essay. But while Knight merely made a passing comment on women and the bourgeoisie according to this story, Hennessy and Mohan take an indepth look at the story for what it means for women. They call the murder of Julia Stoner a "symbolic rape," as the story "dramatizes the sexual economy of patriarchy: the equation of woman and property" (Hennessy and Mohan 390). Essentially, Hennessy and Mohan argue that this story, and many other Sherlock stories, use the patriarchal sexual notions of women to relate them to property. Even further, the women of the story, Roylott's stepdaughters, are related to property by the use of their engagements. Roylott is only at risk of losing money because the daughters are to be married, essentially the money is not even the daughter's but their husband's.

In addition, they point out that Holmes acts as the male savior who protects Julia's sister from the same fate. This is aided by the otherness of the murderer, Roylott. The authors point out that Roylott's association with gypsies and foreign interests paints him the villain, and in opposition of him, Holmes becomes the hero and thus the protector. Hennessy and Mohan continue their argument with discussion of The Married Women's Property Act and the Criminal Law Amendment Act, providing real world political and legal examples to confirm their arguments of women's places in Victorian England and solidify the very real interpretation of women in the Holmes stories. They conclude their arguments by saying "The seme of animal irrationality sexualizes both patriarch-predator and daughter-victim, entangling the feminine...as other in opposition to Holmes's rational, reserved, western, middle-class norm" (Hennessy and Mohan 400).

While all three essays start their analysis of the Sherlock Holmes stories under the same theme, society, they do so in unique ways. Perhaps most different is Knight's essay, as he focuses on the fears and ideologies of the Victorian bourgeoisie. He specifically explores Doyle's use of the scientific method, an important phenomenon of the Victorians and the common fear of disruption in the bourgeoisie home. While Belsey focuses on women, like Hennessy and Mohan, she focuses on what women's presence in the Holmes stories for the scientific method, circling back to a central idea of Knight's argument. Very similar to Belsey, Hennessy and Mohan turn their argument to women and their place in the Holmes stories and Victorian society, but while Knight and Belsey discuss the scientific influence, Hennessy and Mohan consider the political world in their analysis of women's presence. Like Knight, though, they discuss the implications according to the bourgeoisie family.

Together, these essays bring up some of the key components of the Sherlock Holmes stories. On first thought, Sherlock Holmes is an eccentric character who solves intriguing mysteries, but hidden in the lines, these stories hide an even bigger secret, that of the culture of Victorian society. These essays show readers and historians alike the type of world citizens of Victorian England lived in, their hopes and fears, their politics and ideology. From Knight's presentation of the scientific method, to Belsey's further exploration of science in regards to women, to Hennessy and Mohan's overall analysis of women, these essays give readers a new point of view in consideration of the Holmes stories. They are not only fun mysteries solved by a man named Sherlock Holmes and his sidekick Watson, they are an in depth study of the most important aspects to Victorian society.

Works Cited

Belsey, Catherine. "Deconstructing the Text: Sherlock Holmes." *Sherlock Holmes: The Major Stories with Contemporary Critical Essays,* 1994, pp. 381–388.,https://doi.org/10.1007/978-1-349-13419-9_25.

Hennessy, Rosemary, and Rajeswari Mohan. "'The Speckled Band': The Construction of Woman in a Popular Text of Empire." *Sherlock Holmes: The Major Stories with Contemporary Critical Essays,* 1994, pp. 389–401., https://doi.org/10.1007/978-1-349-13419-9_26.

Knight, Stephen. "The Case of the Great Detective." *Sherlock Holmes: The Major Stories with Contemporary Critical Essays,* 1994, pp. 368–380., https://doi.org/10.1007/978-1-349-13419-9_24.

Emily M. Fedon

Riot Grrrl: The Nineties and Now

Feminist movements have come and gone with varying degrees of impact. These movements can form in a variety of ways, including through music. Although flawed, riot grrrl as a music genre was important for feminism, propelling it into the twenty-first century with a punk-flavored punch. Throughout the nineties riot grrrl was a notable feminist movement of the time. However, its impact, even thirty years later, cannot be ignored. Riot grrrl created a powerful culture inspiring change for women that lasted decades past its mainstream popularity.

From its inception, many spellings of the movement exist, and common forms are riot grrl, riot grrrl, and riot girl (McDonnell and Vincentelli). For simplicity's sake, riot grrrl will be used going forward. Now, what is riot grrrl? Rolling Stone has a list of many popular riot grrrl albums, such as Bikini Kill's The Singles, multiple Sleater-Kinney albums, Bratmobile's Pottymouth, Le Tigre's self-titled, Heavens to Betsy's Calculated, and many more (Sheffield). Kathleen Hanna of Bikini Kill began creating zines while she was in college, publishing the riot grrrl manifesto in 1991 in her second zine (Hunt). This manifesto included many ideas that the movement stood for, including a rejection of assimilation, a desire to promote women's work, a hatred of capitalism, anger at a sexist society, and a belief that girls will change the world ("Riot Grrrl Manifesto"). Riot grrrl bluntly expressed its desire to fight against obstacles for women through various forms of art. From the beginning, self-identified riot grrrls worked to make women be heard.

Riot grrrl increased in popularity as the nineties drew on. However, many members were dissatisfied with the media's representation (Hunt). The movement was deemed radical, with members dubbed as violent girls who "terrorized men through their man-hating confessions," which unfairly ties the movement to men rather than women ("Riot Grrrl"). Riot grrrls hated this branding because it is the type of thing that the movement was against: forcing women to only be viewed through the men around them. The women at the forefront of riot grrrl were not always interviewed for publications about the movement, but when they were interviewed, they typically tried to redirect attention to feminist topics that were important but not covered in mainstream media ("Riot Grrrl"). This was more of a struggle in the nineties than it is now, and these views were less accepted. Because of its anti-establishment takes, it makes sense that riot grrrl would not do well in mass media and even be misconstrued. Over the years, the criticism affected the movement, and it did not last long in the mainstream (McDonnell and Vincentelli). Despite its short time in the spotlight, the movement has been able to preserve itself and continue influencing generations of girls since the nineties.

Although some have said that riot grrrl is dead, the original bands are still finding success. Original riot grrrl band Bikini Kill will embark on a North American tour in 2023 with support from different bands for different dates, including Mannequin Pussy, Hurry Up, H.C. McEntire, and other punk bands (Kress). This lineup includes female punk acts that began in the nineties and female punk bands that are only a few years old. Additionally, Le Tigre will go on their first tour in almost twenty years this summer, with some shows already selling out (Ruiz). This year's Mosswood Meltdown will feature riot grrrl pioneers Bratmobile and Le Tigre as well ("Mosswood Meltdown"). These numerous original riot grrrl bands touring around the same time should not be seen as a coincidence. People are rediscovering these bands and the genre itself, and it has gained some popularity in recent years.

Since this is the digital age, apps like Tik Tok have been useful in the modernization of the original riot grrrl. Women and non-binary people have been making videos about the fashion, music, and history of the movement ("Can Riot Grrrl Tik Tok Re-Imagine a Flawed Scene?"). However, the resurgence is fueled by more than just aesthetic and art; many feminist topics that were popular in the nineties have gained relevance again in the past few years ("Can Riot Grrrl Tik Tok Re-Imagine a Flawed Scene?"). Attacks on a woman's right to choose and discussions about the prevalence of rape culture in society are just two examples of feminist subjects that were popular now and then. Anti-establishment ideas are also currently popular amid discussions of the struggle of living through late-stage capitalism and the climate crisis. Along with a love of the music and the culture, many women and non-binary people also want to advocate for a better future for everyone, regardless of gender.

Nostalgia plays another big role in the increased popularity of many parts of twentieth-century culture, including riot grrrl. People are not looking back with rose-colored glasses though, and amid the appreciation for the work of riot grrrl there has been some criticism. One of the major criticisms is how the feminism presented by riot grrrl is mostly "white feminism," which does not attempt to help women who are part of other minority groups, such as trans women and women of color. In the nineties, many women of color felt "left out of the movement" and that "it was just for white women" (Demir). The resurgence of riot grrrl in the twenty-first century acknowledges this downfall of the original movement and seeks to stay true to feminist ideas while promoting intersectionality, with many online movements helping to accomplish this goal (Demir). This modernization of the movement helps to keep riot grrrl alive while making it more accessible and safer for more groups of people.

With an awareness of the importance of intersectional feminism, people bringing back riot grrrl have been vocal about wanting to include more than only white, cis, middle-class, suburban women, and they have included sista grrrl in their conversations about riot grrrl ("Can Riot Grrrl Tik Tok Re-Imagine a Flawed Scene?"). Sista grrrl was a movement in response to the lack of racial inclusivity of riot grrrl, and it was created for women of color who also wanted to find a community in the punk scene (Demir). Those seeking to bring back the riot grrrl movement today want to make sure that this sort of divergence isn't necessary for people to feel included. The reinvention of riot grrrl allows the movement to live on while creating needed change to right the wrongs of the past. Current feminist, anti-establishment, and intersectional discourse can find itself in the new version of riot grrrl.

Since it began in 1991, riot grrrl has inspired change in young women who have found the movement. While it originally lasted for a few years in the nineties, it never completely died. Even thirty years after it first began, riot grrrl is still popular with the current generation of young women. Primarily through online communities, these women have been circulating information about the art, music, history, and flaws of riot grrrl. Through this recent popularization of the movement, the new generation has been finding ways to fight against its shortcomings and be accessible to a wider demographic of people. As women's rights are still attacked today, such as the Supreme Court decision to overturn *Roe v. Wade,* riot grrrl has been a way for women to find a community to fight against the unfairness. The legacy of riot grrrl continues to live on as it is brought back into an intersectional feminist movement. As long as there is inequality between people of all genders, riot grrrl will likely still be around for those who will loudly and unapologetically demand equality.

Works Cited

"Can Riot Grrrl Tik Tok Re-Imagine a Flawed Scene?" *Billboard.* August 13, 2021. https://www.billboard.com/music/rock/riot-grrrl-tiktok-revival-9614584/. Date Accessed: March 1, 2023.

Demir, Emia. "Riot Grrrl: A Critique of 90s Punk Feminism." *unpublished magazine.* February 18, 2021. https://www.unpublishedzine.com/music/riot-grrrl-a-critique-of-90s-punk-feminism. Date Accessed: March 1, 2023.

Hunt, El. "A Brief History of Riot Grrrl–the Space-Reclaiming 90s Punk Movement." *NME* August 27, 2019. https://www.nme.com/blogs/nme-blogs/brief-history-riot-grrrl-space-reclaiming-90s-punk-movement-2542166. Date Accessed: March 1, 2023.

Kress, Brian. "Bikini Kill Announces 2023 Tour Support with Mannequin Pussy, HC McEntire, and More." *Consequence.* November 17, 2022. https://consequence.net/2022/11/bikini-kill-2023-tour-dates-support/. Date Accessed: March 1, 2023.

McDonnell, Evelyn, Vincentelli, Elisabeth. "Riot Grrrl United Feminism and Punk. Here's an Essential Listening Guide." *New York Times.* May 6, 2019. https://www.nytimes.com/interactive/2019/05/03/arts/music/riot-grrrl-playlist.html. Date Accessed: March 1, 2023.

"Mosswood Meltdown." *Mosswood Meltdown.* https://mosswoodmeltdown.com. Date Accessed: March 1, 2023.

"Riot Grrrl." *Grinnell College.* https://haenfler.sites.grinnell.edu/subcultures-and-scenes/riot-grrrl-2/. Date Accessed: March 1, 2023.

"Riot Grrrl Manifesto." *History is a Weapon.* https://www.historyisaweapon.com/defcon1/riotgrrrlmanifesto.html. Date Accessed: March 1, 2023.

Ruiz, Matthew Ismael. "Le Tigre Announce First Tour in Nearly 20 Years." *Pitchfork.* January 24, 2023. https://pitchfork.com/news/le-tigre-announce-first-tour-in-nearly-20-years/. Date Accessed: March 1, 2023

Sheffield, Rob. "Riot Grrrl Album Guide." *Rolling Stone.* March 27, 2020. https://www.rollingstone.com/music/music-lists/riot-grrrl-album-guide-bikini-kill-sleater-kinney-972476/wild-flag-romance-2011-972600/. Date Accessed: March 1, 2023.

Grace Fisher
Lönnrot's *Kalevala:* A National Myth

In an article for the Finnish Literature Society, folklorist Urpo Vento asks, "Is there any other book in world literature like the *Kalevala,* which has had such a profound impact on its original language and which has become to the same degree a source of identity symbols?" (91). The *Iliad* and the *Odyssey* may come to mind, but nonetheless it is hard to overstate the importance of the *Kalevala,* which was instrumental in both the development of Finnish as a language and Finland as a nation. To this day, "*Kalevala* Day" is marked in Finland every year on Feb. 28th as a celebration of Finnish culture. First published by Elias Lönnrot in 1835, the epic is a compilation of folk songs and poems originally set to music that Lönnrot collected from around Finland. Together the poems, divided into twenty-four Runes, form one narrative. To what extent the epic is authentic myth and to what extent it was created by Lönnrot has long been up for debate. Many scholars believe that, although Lönnrot wrote little of the actual text of the *Kalevala* himself, the cohesive narrative formed by the poems is largely his creation (Dukes).

Some of the outsize impact of the *Kalevala* was doubtless due to the circumstances in which it was published (which Lönnrot was, of course, aware of when he wrote); in 1835, the tide of nationalism was rising in Europe, and the Finnish people were seeking to define their own identity. The *Kalevala* written in Finnish was crucial to the formation of national identity in a society where the upper class spoke Swedish, "the language of science was still Latin, and Russian was required in the administration" (Vetno 85). Later, the *Kalevala* was used as a political tool by both the Soviet Union and Finnish nationalists who opposed the Russification of Finland, which further contributed to its fame (Vihavainen). But though it had been primed for success by extratextual factors, the *Kalevala* is undeniably a beautiful poem and worthy of study both in its own right and as a resource for Finnish myth. None of our ancient records of myth were written from a disinterested standpoint (if such a thing exists). Even if Lönnrot's organization of the separate texts and his intention to promote Finnish culture form a large part of it, this makes the *Kalevala* no more inauthentic than the *Metamorphoses* of Ovid, who wrote to entertain, or the *Prose Edda* of Snorri Sturluson, who wrote to show Christianity's superiority over, as well as to preserve, the Norse mythological system. The creation story of the *Kalevala,* which is told mostly in the first Rune, is a good illustration of the way Lönnrot's aims are evident in the *Kalevala,* as well as of the beauty of the poem itself.

The poem begins not with action, but with a brief preface from the point of view of a bard: "I am ready now for singing / Ready now to begin the chanting / Of our nation's ancient folk-song / Handed down from by-gone ages" (1). The narrator later continues, "These my dear old father sang me ... These my tender mother taught me" (2). It's not unusual for a mythical work to begin with an explanation of its origin and authority (or lack thereof, as with Sturluson's explanation of how the legends of the Norse gods had grown up around famous heroes who were once mortal men), but what is interesting here is which aspect's veracity is emphasized: not the truth of the myths themselves, but their real origin as authentic myths of the Finnish people passed down verbally through the generations. Lönnrot is not trying to convert anyone to the traditional Finnish belief system; in a Finland that was thoroughly either secular or Christian, that cause was already lost (though Lönnrot's lack of any Christian references is deliberate, as he was trying to convincingly record pre-Christian verse). Rather Lönnrot was emphasizing the existence of a uniquely Finnish history and culture. To some extent, the myth Lönnrot really cared about persuading his audience of was the historical existence of the nation of Finland.

Many old-world creation stories share common elements. Knowing this, Lönnrot likely felt no obligation, when arranging the folksongs he had gathered, to remove elements from other belief systems, even though he was both retelling and creating a uniquely Finnish system. Creation in the *Kalevala* begins with Ilmatar, "Beauteous Daughter of the Ether," descending to the ocean; previously she had lived in a heaven-like plane (5). As in the Babylonian *Enuma Elish* and the Priestly writer's parts of Genesis, waters are primeval; there is no creation out of nothing, and the first source of life is female, followed by a more powerful male figure—in the *Kalevala*, Väinämöinen.

A more striking similarity is with the Iroquois myth of creation, which also begins with a woman descending from heaven into a watery universe before the creation of earth; in the Iroquois myth this woman's daughter is impregnated by the wind, as Ilmatar is in the *Kalevala*. Interestingly, one of the earliest existing accounts of the Iroquois myth was recorded in the 1880s by the ethnographer Jeremiah Curtin, who twenty years before had learned Finnish while studying modern languages at Harvard and so would probably have been familiar with the *Kalevala*; but assuming that both Curtin and Lönnrot were reasonably faithful in their recordings, the similarities seem to be a coincidence (or, if you are not of a skeptical nature, evidence for Jung's theories of a collective unconscious—or even for Rank's theory of the hero myth; after all, Väinämöinen is born of a virgin and passes through water) (Murphy).

After Ilmatar's descent to the watery world, she swims through the ocean for hundreds of years in labor. Eventually a duck flies down, rests on her knee, and lays eggs from which the world is created. Väinämöinen is also born. Ilmatar's movements through the water (reminiscent of the Babylonian goddess Tiamat's role in the Babylonian creation myth) also help create the world: "Where she turned in water / There arose a fertile hillock; / Whereso'er her foot she rested / There she made a hole for fishes" (10). Väinämöinen escapes the ocean and walks on dry land; later, he will plant the forests. Väinämöinen will be the great Finnish hero of the epic; Vento argues that Lönnrot envisioned him as "the last receding figure of the heathen age" (83).

It's a cohesive story, with few of the paratactical contradictions common to oral poetry. This is consistent with Lönnrot's aim; the more sophisticated the *Kalevala* was, the more "the Finns were elevated to the same level as the other nations, which had created their national eposés" (Vihavainen). Still, as is common in oral poetry, the *Kalevala* assumes previous knowledge in the listener of the story it tells: Väinämöinen's birth is never described, and we're never actually told that he is the same child that Ilmatar bore; even Ilmatar herself is named only in the last line of Rune 1. Despite Lönnrot's organization and editing—and it's difficult to know just how extensive that was—the *Kalevala* is essentially authentic and remains a valuable repository of Finnish mythology.

Works Cited

Crawford, John Martin, translator. *The Kalevala.* By Elias Lönnrot, Cinncinnati: the Robert Clarke Company, 1898.

Dukes, Hunter. "English Translation of Finland's Epic Poem, the Kalevala (1898) Introductory Text." *The Public Domain Review*, 2021, https://publicdomainreview.org/collection/kalevala.

Murphy, Maureen. "Curtin, Jeremiah." *Curtin, Jeremiah* | Dictionary of Irish Biography, 2009, https://www.dib.ie/biography/curtin-jeremiah-a2329.

Thury, Eva M., and Margaret Klopfle Devinney. *Introduction to Mythology: Contemporary Approaches to Classical and World Myth*s. Oxford University Press, 2017.

Vento, Urpo. "The Role of the Kalevala in Finnish Culture and Politics." *Nordic Journal of African Studies*, vol. 1, no. 2, 1992, pp. 82-93. http://www.njas.helsinki.fi/pdf-files/vol1num2/vento.pdf.

Vihavainen, Timo. "To Whom Does the Kalevala Belong?" *Books from Finland*, 1999, http://neba.finlit.fi/booksfromfinland/bff/299/vihavainen.htm.

Annette Kroes

Consumerism and Climate: The Intersection of Environmental Guilt and Responsibility

For the sake of the argument, picture the following hypothetical situation: you are scrolling through Instagram while eating a meal between classes, and you come across a picture of trash packed tightly into a glass jar or a plastic bottle, or a Ziploc bag. What you are likely seeing is a zero-waste content creator's trash accumulation over the course of a year or more. Let's also say you're the average American, who, according to the Environmental Protection Agency, produces approximately 4.9 pounds of trash each day ("National Overview..."). Realistically, one jar's worth of trash over the course of an entire year seems ridiculous. But if these internet strangers can limit their waste in such productive ways, why can't you? We know the answer: that lifestyle might be unattainable at the moment, or uninteresting to you, but even still, the plastic coffee cup in your non-scrolling hand might just be feeling the tiniest bit heavier. Whether or not you resonate with this, this feeling of environmental guilt is a very real problem for a lot of regular consumers.

Let's revisit our hypothetical Instagram feed: you'll encounter islands of garbage in the ocean, insurmountable landfills, and crowded highways on your scrolling journey. How can we deny the guilt we feel looking at the Earth degraded, when we each undeniably contribute to it? Is each one of us ethically responsible for the destruction caused by our inevitable consumption? Take a breath and a break from the doom-scrolling, because the answer is no: society's overconsumption leads to a feeling of environmental guilt, but due to our positions as consumers, the guilt we feel does not directly equate to the ethical responsibility we owe to the environment.

Environmental guilt can plague consumers whenever they prioritize convenience or comfort over the most sustainable choice they are aware of. Sarah Fredricks explains this concept in her work, "Evidence of Environmental Guilt and Shame." An excerpt from this piece examines blog posts of environmentalists and ecologically concerned citizens committing what they refer to as "eco-sins" (Fredricks). Whether it's forgetting a reusable bag, letting the hot water run, or leaving the back door open with the air conditioning on, these people end up feeling as if they've committed a crime. Fredricks surmised that these posters "desire something else—to feel differently, particularly about themselves." Everyday environmentalists, as Fredricks calls them, feel more obligated to a sense of perfection as opposed to progress (Fredricks 28). By prioritizing the desire to feel guiltless, consumers miss the opportunity to take pride in the changes they have made, reevaluate their lives to see what else they can do, or gain the confidence to educate others. It is difficult to be perfect in an industrial world—as Fredricks later says, "the system, not the species, is flawed" (Fredricks 35). To avoid these feelings of inadequacy while also making an active change, those negative feelings should be repurposed as pride for feeling the agency to make a change, rather than succumbing to the discouragement and hopelessness of guilt.

It isn't that easy, though, and those who can relate to the hypothetical from earlier know this from experience. While consumers may try to purchase the right products, with kinder labels and more efficient packaging, the entire market of sustainability can be ambiguous. Suppliers make labels confusing on purpose, as consumers are more likely to purchase something that presents itself as environmentally friendly. GreenPrint, a global environmental technology company that measures sustainability goals for companies, conducted a survey on consumers and eco-friendly products and reported the results in their March 2021 Business of Sustainability Index. It found that "77% of Americans are concerned about the environmental impact of products they buy." The same study stated that although 64% of Americans are willing to pay more for products that appear to be sustainable, 74% do not know how to identify such products ("GreenPrint Survey Finds..."). People are more concerned with making eco-conscious decisions, but they are also less likely, and oftentimes are not expected, to verify the claims made by these companies. Marketers know these things, and if there is a way to appeal to consumers' desire to shop from sustainable businesses, while also avoiding the extra costs incurred by truly becoming one of such, that is the most profitable avenue.

Greenwashing, in the words of UCLA Professor Magali A. Delmas and former PhD student Vanessa Cuerel Burbano, is "misleading consumers about firm environmental performance or the environmental benefits of a product or service." An article published in 2019 in the *Journal of Business Ethics* claims that firms may be getting away with greenwashing due to the blindness consumers experience when it comes to supply-chain affairs. The authors of the article explain that greenwashing "may take place when a company declares itself to be socially and environmentally responsible, yet engages in a relationship with a supplier who pollutes the environment, or mistreats its employees" (Pizzetti et al). If the problems are happening outside of regulatory control and consumer knowledge, the consumer cannot always be expected to make the right decision. The ambiguity and misinformation within the market make it difficult to begin to frame one's impact on the environment, leading to confusion and skepticism in the sustainable market.

"Zero-waste" and "low-waste" movements have surfaced out of the debate of environmental responsibility as other possible solutions to overconsumption. The idea is this: if the production market is ambiguous and wasteful, changing the consumer lifestyle to one that avoids overconsuming altogether is the most realistic sustainable avenue. However, to live waste-free is not an accessible option for all. On one hand, zero-waste living is hard to achieve. As stated by Alexandra Aladham, a student of Oxford College, "Although many environmentalists and zero waste lifestyle followers only intend to better the world through their actions and beliefs, some overlook the importance of varied perspectives and mindsets." Using the example of individuals with disabilities, Aladham highlights that what may be wasteful products to some are necessary tools to others. Examples like this include plastic utensils, such as straws or forks, which were removed from many restaurants and stores across America in recent years (Aladham). On the other hand, these products were invented for the purpose of being convenient and affordable. Few people are willing, and less people are able, to sacrifice convenience or affordability for ethics. This does not negate the zero-waste movement as a valid and accessible alternative for some, but it does prove that it is not a solution for all. Alternatively, it may be intuitive to encourage zero-waste living as a jumping-off point, allowing consumers to make changes that accommodate their lives. When conscious and practical sustainable choices are made, instead of exclusively absolving oneself of guilt, the impact is much larger and much more attainable for the consumer.

For sustainable lifestyle changes to have an impact they must be meaningful, educated choices that are personally tailored to each individual life. Holding consumers to a standard of perfection is counterintuitive because it hinders room for improvement and limits the ability to appreciate realistic progress. However, on the other side, relinquishing all environmental responsibility is not the solution. We should not feel ethically challenged when living life the way we have to, but this doesn't mean we owe absolutely no responsibility to the environment, reducing consumption, and ignoring the looming threat of climate change. To sum it up, there is no one-size-fits-all parameter we all must follow. Due to our positions as consumers and the vastly different lifestyles we all lead, plus the fact that sustainability can be ambiguous and inaccessible, there is no productive reason to feel guilty about our choices. The best thing we can do is recognize what changes we can make, understand the ones we cannot, and acknowledge our progress as we move toward a cleaner future, together.

Works Cited

Aladham, Alexandra. "Zero Waste Ambassador Blog: Eco-Ableism in the Zero Waste Movement." https://sustainability.emory.edu/eco-ableism-in-the-zero-waste-movement/. Accessed 14 November 2022.

Delmas, Magali A., and Vanessa Cuerel Burbano. "The Drivers of Greenwashing." *California Management Review*, vol. 54, no. 1, 2011, pp. 64–87, https://doi.org/10.1525/cmr.2011.54.1.64. Accessed 2 December 2022.

Fredericks, Sarah E., "Evidence of Environmental Guilt and Shame', Environmental Guilt and Shame: Signals of Individual and Collective Responsibility and the Need for Ritual Responses" *(Oxford, 2021, online edn, Oxford Academic, 22 July 2021)*, https://doi-org.ezproxy2.library.drexel.edu/10.1093/oso/9780198042699.003.0002, accessed 2 Nov. 2022.

"GreenPrint Survey Finds Consumers Want to Buy Eco-Friendly Products, but Don't Know How to Identify them." *Business Wire*, Mar 22, 2021. ProQuest, http://ezproxy2.library.drexel.edu/login?url=https://www-proquest-com.ezproxy2.library.drexel.edu/wire-feeds/greenprint-survey-finds-consumers-want-buy-eco/docview/2503400846/se-2. Accessed 14 November 2022.

"National Overview: Facts and Figures on Materials, Wastes and Recycling." *EPA*, Environmental Protection Agency, https://www.epa.gov/facts-and-figures-about-materials-waste-and-recycling/national-overview-facts-and-figures-materials. Accessed 1 December 2022.

Pizzetti, Marta, et al. "Firms Talk, Suppliers Walk: Analyzing the Locus of Greenwashing in the Blame Game and Introducing 'Vicarious Greenwashing.'" *Journal of Business Ethics*, vol. 170, no. 1, 2021, pp. 21–38, https://doi.org/10.1007/s10551-019-04406-2. Accessed 2 December 2022.

Elaria Mousa
Education: A Change of Priorities

In a perfect world, everyone would have access to education. No matter where you live, who you are, or how much money you make, education should be not only available but also beneficial. In reality, in our imperfect world, this is not the case. That is why 22 years ago, my parents made the decision to immigrate from Egypt to the United States. They wanted to make sure that their children had the best education possible. However, this wasn't a unique experience for my parents. Millions of parents across the globe were abandoning their homeland and starting a new life in America because of how much they valued education. This was an extremely difficult, draining, and painful decision to make for both the immigrants and their families they may be leaving behind. The trauma of moving to a new country with a language barrier and no friends or family solely to give your children better opportunities translated into astronomically high expectations. While having high expectations is not always a bad thing, the pressure that was placed on my shoulders to become a high-achieving student was detrimental both physically and mentally. Mental health should be prioritized in students' education experiences, especially those with immigrant parents.

A good education was of the utmost importance to my parents—important enough to move across the globe for. They felt that because they had completely uprooted their life and immigrated, they needed to bear the fruit of their labor; this fruit being academically successful children. However, "good education" in their eyes, and the eyes of many other parents, really meant "good grades." This is because "the United States has been reliant on quantitative assessments to measure success" (Rivero). Without growing up in America and understanding the school system, quantitative data was the only thing these parents had to assess their child's success. The process of achieving these good grades and what was sacrificed on the way was never acknowledged. The only thing that mattered was a report card with a plethora of A+s and a ranking at the top of the class, preferably valedictorian. As a result of this, many students exerted themselves to the maximum and sacrificed their mental and physical health in order to please their parents. Many studies were conducted on how grades affected the well-being of students, and it was found that "worse than expected grades affected daily self-esteem and this dependent relationship between grades and self-worth seems to have greater costs than benefits for students" (Ruppert). Due to the constant praise of high grades and the disappointment associated with moderate or low grades, many students began to base their self-worth on the marks they received. From my experience and speaking with my peers throughout the years, I have found that many first-generation students are raised to be achievement-oriented individuals because their parents want to see their kids accomplish what they could not. Both I and many of my family members and friends were raised believing that we had to become doctors, lawyers, engineers, etc., to be successful, and in order to do this, we had to do well in school. Students raised with this achievement-oriented mindset "are hungry for tracking progress toward the achievement of academic goals, and grades satisfy those ends" (Ruppert). As we grow older, these expectations not only become our parents' but also ours. As a result, when we receive a bad grade, it becomes a reflection of self-worth instead of a way to grow.

While it may feel like it, this extreme academic pressure from immigrant parents is not unique to a few selected students. This issue ranges across many students from many different cultural backgrounds. Although there may be a difference in cultural background, studies have shown that many immigrants share the same experiences of acclimating to a new environment (Bismar), and "college students from immigrant families are likely brought up with different communication and relationship-maintenance patterns from those typically seen in the United States" (Bismar). In my experience, many of my peers with immigrant parents shared the same struggles that I did, while those with non-immigrant parents usually could not relate to the mindset and expectations we had, mostly due to the culture in which we grew up in. This culture, personally, was also one that had a severe stigma around mental health. Mental health was seen as a concept that was associated with weak people and those who couldn't handle their lives better. The issue with this is that very often the overbearing, perfectionist expectations enforced on the students caused mental health issues (Bismar). As I discussed before, grades became a reflection of self-worth, so when grades were not up to par with the expectation, this often led to depressive states and anxiety. A study was done that showed that "compared with their White American peers, immigrants and individuals who grew up in immigrant families tend to possess more mental illness (MI) stigma and harbor greater negativity toward seeking professional help" (Bismar). There was a pattern seen in the poor mental health of students with immigrant parents and the lack of ability to seek help or cope with these issues because of the stigma surrounding mental health in many cultures. This can lead to a downward spiral of the mental health of students already at such a vulnerable age, and it can begin to affect their physical and psychological health.

What I have learned from my experience is that academic success is not linear and cannot be quantified by the grades I receive. Both I and many of my peers understand how damaging hyper-focusing on grades as a measure of success can be, which is why there should be an active effort to reverse these expectations for the next generation of students. The first step to this is trying to change our individual mindsets from what we were brought up with. We first have to acknowledge and embrace our failures in order to be able to do this for others. Personally, this was one of the biggest obstacles for me. I had to rewire my brain into accepting failure and using it as a stepping stone for growth. In addition to this, we must educate others on the effects of such unrealistic expectations, especially parents and elders who may have enforced these expectations without realizing the repercussions. We also need to advocate for the mental health of ourselves, our peers, and future students. While it may be difficult, the only way to truly solve this issue is to destigmatize seeking help. This will be especially difficult in cultures that reject this idea completely, but in a study done on introducing mental health topics in the Middle East, it was found that the best approach to a more mental-health-friendly environment was educating families on how to support their loved ones in overcoming shame and seeking treatment, and also educating young people (Sewilman, *et al.*). It is our responsibility as the upcoming generation of contributors to society to not make the same mistakes our parents did and provide an environment that fosters care and support to those who come after us so that they don't have to suffer in the same ways we did.

Works Cited

Bismar, Danna. "Mental Illness Stigma and Help-Seeking Attitudes of Students With Immigrant Parents." *Journal of College Counseling*, Jun. 2021, https://onlinelibrary-wiley-com.ezproxy2.library.drexel.edu/doi/full/10.1002/jocc.12182.

Rivero, Ayumi. Review of Hyper Education: *Why Good Schools, Good Grades, and Good Behavior Are Not Enough*, by Pawan Dhingra. May 2022, https://journals-sagepub-com.ezproxy2.library.drexel.edu/doi/full/10.1177/23326492221103630.

Ruppert, Bryan. "Grade Expectations: When 100% Isn't Good Enough." *Journal of Management Education*, Nov. 2020, https://journals-sagepub-com.ezproxy2.library.drexel.edu/doi/full/10.1177/1052562920964515.

Sewilam, Ahmed M, et al. "Suggested Avenues to Reduce the Stigma of Mental Illness in the Middle East." *The International Journal of Social Psychiatry*, Mar. 2015, https://www.ncbi.nlm.nih.gov/pmc/articles/PMC4852850/.

Brooke Thompson
Art Triggering Environmental Change

The world today is viewed as being in one of the most socially aware and culturally conscious states it has ever been in. Without a doubt, recent years have seen heightened awareness for social and political issues. However, while people may be aware and concerned with these topics, there is little action being done. This is especially true with climate change. Often, the public does not know how to make a change and/or isn't motivated enough to do so; this needs to change in order for any environmental dilemma to be solved or, at the very least, lessened. This is where the arts come in. Perhaps a less conventional approach could be what inspires people to become devoted to the cause and implement *actual* activism. Because more effort from the public is needed to make a difference in the current state of the environment, looking into different ways to move people to action is incredibly important. The arts have inspired people and stirred great emotions for millennia; surely they could inspire a few people to care more about the environment around them. The use of art visualizations can effectively motivate people to take a more active role in addressing environmental concerns. Art can act as a powerful aid in fighting environmental problems by promoting environmentally friendly practices and inspiring people to act.

It may be argued that the inspiring effect of art is not nearly enough to move people to save the planet. The encoding/decoding model of communication says otherwise. Developed by renowned cultural theorist and sociologist Stuart Hall in 1973, the encoding/decoding model explains the relationship between a sender of a message and its recipient. Hall was focused on the distortion a message may go through before it gets to the recipient, based on the means of sending it. In his 1973 report titled "Encoding and Decoding in the Television Discourse," Hall concluded that there is a "lack of fit between the codes [of sender and recipient]." Lack of fit can be defined as the "gap" between how a message is presented and how it is received; there is some wiggle room for interpretation (Hall). Art can capitalize on this lack of fit by acting as the encoder; a piece of art causes its viewers or recipients to engage, interact with, and decode its message. This is an extremely powerful way to transfer ideas of environmental urgency because art forces people to decode, think, and become inspired by its messages. This produces a much more personal (and therefore powerful) effect on viewers, as opposed to the effect they'd get simply by reading a stale, visually lacking research article.

As explored above, the real power of the arts lies in their ability to inspire and move. People are much more receptive to messages conveyed through art as opposed to boring, mundane factual articles. In their article, "Visualizing climate change: an exploratory study of the effectiveness of artistic information visualizations," researchers Ulrike Hahn and Pauwke Berkers ask, "How can the general public be effectively engaged beyond awareness?" To them, the answer lies in the arts. Throughout their article and experiment, Hahn and

Berkers explored the degree to which different types of media made viewers consider climate change as important. They did this by providing participants with multiple visuals, and then conducting surveys, interviews, and a q-sort (a method of sorting information based on what the experiment asks; in this case, sorting visuals based on whether they conveyed climate change as important). They found that overall, "less abstract" and "clearer" AIVs (artistic information visualizations) were more effective in getting viewers to accept climate change as an important issue. Unsurprisingly, more complicated pieces of art that needed a higher degree of art education were found to be less effective due to the average person not possessing an extensive amount of art knowledge (Hahn and Berkers). Artist Jill Pelto uses the reflection in sunglasses and graphical lines to portray her message about global warming (Pelto). Minute details like these may be missed by the majority.

The overall finding of the experiment was that digital photos (classified as a type of visual art) *paired* with news sources are the most effective in producing feelings that climate change is an important issue. By adding visuals to scientific articles or newscasts, the audience can pair the important facts being presented to them with a visual that invokes emotion.

Hahn and Berkers' experiment provides a direct measure of how engaging different types of visual art can be, which quantitatively shows the power of the arts. People need to be powered by something in order to be moved into acting for it, and this data shows exactly which types of art were the most inspiring. As seen in the experiment, factual reports coupled with visualizations can result in greater concern and connect viewers with the issue at hand. This is what *needs* to happen in order for any sort of activism to take place. Hahn and Berkers state that while art can "compliment the scientific narrative," it can also inspire hope for a better environmental future. Art is the key to kickstarting the action needed to bring about superior climate-friendly times.

While the benefits described so far have been some indirect effects by art, art can also directly help the ecosystem. Trash and pollution are two main sources of environmental harm. Researchers Estelle Castro-Koshy and Geraldine Le Roux apply an artistic look to this problem in their article titled, "Indigenous Art and Sovereignty Inspiring Change against Environmental Degradation." They state that the main goal they had in researching and composing this article was to "explore artistic approaches deployed in or around spaces faced with...pollution and waste." Specifically, in Le Roux's studies, she observed a "redefinition of plastic from waste" in the form of local Indigenous artists taking ghost nets and repurposing them into giant, artistic sculptures. These ghost nets—fishermen's nets that have been abandoned and cast out into the environment—can be extremely dangerous to marine life and the ecosystem (Stelfox). Smaller pieces of these nets and other similar plastic/acrylic materials can also disintegrate into the dreaded micro plastics (Lebreton et al.). By getting these harmful materials out of the ecosystem, the trash cannot break down and further pollute the environment. Additionally, nets that can entangle and suffocate already endangered marine life (such as sea turtles or the vaquita—a type of porpoise (World Wildlife Fund Inc.) are removed.

These artistic practices and art forms resulted in the removal of harmful pollutants from the environment, encouraged locals to help collect trash for the art, and added culturally rich sculptures to the community. These are invaluable benefits and examples of how art can lead to activities that greatly aid in the fight for environmental conservation.

Art allows people to have *fun* and feel good about helping the environment, while also inspiring them in ways direct facts can't. The world does not need another blog post about global warming; simple newscasts and commentary are not enough to move people to go pick up trash or use more paper straws. Going forward, we can support small artists trying to advance important social topics. Check out that climate-centered art gallery. Take a little sibling or child out for a nature walk and pick up discarded bottles; create a fun craft with them! Consuming art as opposed to direct information will feel like a breath of fresh air and can provide new perspectives about this issue. Let's use art to teach about and help the climate in unconventional ways—its impact will reach much further.

Works Cited

Castro-Koshy, Estelle, and Le Roux, Géraldine. "Indigenous Art and Sovereignty Inspiring Change against Environmental Degradation." *ETropic: Electronic Journal of Studies in the Tropics*, vol. 19, no. 1, 2020, https://doi.org/10.25120/etropic.19.1.2020.3737.

Hahn, Ulrike and Berkers, Pauwke. "Visualizing climate change: an exploratory study of the effectiveness of artistic information visualizations." *World Art*, 2021, pp. 95- 119, DOI: 10.1080/21500894.2020.1769718.

Hall, Stuart. "Encoding and Decoding in the Television Discourse [Originally 1973; Republished 2007]." *Essential Essays, Volume 1*, 2018, pp. 257–276., https://doi.org/10.2307/j.ctv11cw7c7.16.

Lebreton, Laurent C., van der Zwet, Joost., Damsteeg, Jan-Willem., Slat, Boyan., Andrady, Anthony., & Reisser, Julia. "River Plastic Emissions to the World's Oceans." *Nature Communications*, vol. 8, no. 1, 2017, https://doi.org/10.1038/ncomms15611.

Pelto, Jill. "Moments of Observation." *Jillpelto.com* (2015). https://www.jillpelto.com/moments-of-observation. Accessed 25 Nov. 2022.

Stelfox, Martin. "Untangling the Origin of Ghost Gear within the Maldivian Archipelago and Its Impact on Olive Ridley (Lepidochelys Olivacea) Populations." *Endangered Species Research*, vol. 40, 2019, pp. 309–320., https://doi.org/10.3354/esr00990.

World Wildlife Fund Inc. "Species List." *WWF*, World Wildlife Fund, https://www.worldwildlife.org/species-categories/marine-animals/species/directory.

First Place—The Zelda Provenzano Endowed STEM Writing Award

Keira Earley

Climate Change and the People of the Atlantic Coast

My father's family had a house in Lavalette, a small beach town on the coast of New Jersey, bought when they first immigrated to America. The house had many upgrades over the years but stood in the same place, in the same family for almost a century. When Hurricane Sandy hit in October 2012, I remember hearing my parents read moment-to-moment updates on the damage done to the town: when the power went out, when the bridge my dad took every summer collapsed, when the main road flooded and closed. The silence of my dad's grief in the following days, while we prepared for the storm in our own home in southwest Jersey, was deafening. After a few months had passed, we were finally able to visit. The entire neighborhood was destroyed, as well as all the businesses my dad frequented as a child. The ice cream store he worked at every summer through middle and high school was blown away, along with the boardwalk it resided on. We went into a local pizza place for lunch, and on the wall was a mark of how high the water flooded the building during the storm. At the time of the visit, I was eight years old and around four feet tall. The line was well above my head. Over four feet of water in every home, office, and restaurant in the town.

When news sources or social media spread information or engage in discussions about climate change, they often focus on the plants and animals affected by the changing environment. Updates on the list of endangered and extinct species are shared across platforms very quickly because manipulating users' emotions guarantees more clicks on their articles and more money in their pockets. However, the effects of climate change on *people* are often overlooked. As the threat of climate change continues to grow, people who live in coastal communities face the unpredictability of the shifting environment firsthand. Those living in poverty in these communities also face unequal access to resources needed, such as travel, proper insurance, and medical attention.

For the purpose of this paper, the focus will stay on those affected on the Atlantic Coast. The absence of information on other coasts globally does not imply the absence of similar issues; instead, it introduces one aspect of the conversation of a much broader problem.

Over the past few decades, the threat of hurricanes has increased on the Atlantic Coast of America. According to a study published in the journal *Geophysical Research Letters,* where many climate researchers studied oceanic storms between 1979 and 2018, the average intensification of hurricanes increased by approximately 1.4 miles per hour every six hours on the Atlantic Coast. Compared to forty years ago, hurricanes are becoming stronger and faster above waters close to the coast in significantly less time today, demonstrated by this rise in acceleration. Thus, the unpredictability of storms increases, as the paths originally forecasted for them, when forming over the ocean, greatly shift once nearing the coast. The study produced models for hurricane rates between 2015-2100, providing results that pointed to further increasing of hurricanes intensifying over these 86 years. In addition, the sea surface temperature of waters near the coast increased by almost a third of a degree Celsius on the northeastern coast of America between 1979 and 2018. Temperatures rising at this rate offsets the ocean currents, affecting the winds above these waves, including the Labrador Sea Current (Balaguru et al.). Many processes of the Atlantic Ocean rely on this current because it transfers oxygen from the atmosphere into the water at one of the fastest rates globally than any other section of the ocean (Withers). When the Labrador Sea Current retreats, it affects the molecular makeup of the water in the region, leading to a disruptive feedback loop. Hurricanes are becoming more and more dangerous at faster rates, leaving more people at risk. The combination of stronger winds and unusual ocean currents produces deadly results during hurricane season.

Further, a group of scientists at Harvard researched the flood risk of Atlantic and Gulf Coast hospitals in the US as a part of a *GeoHealth* journal. Hospitals, just like any other building, are not impenetrable to storms. In only the top ten most at-risk hospitals analyzed, tens of thousands of beds were deemed at risk of flooding due to a potential Category 2 storm. 77.6% of hospitals in the Miami-Fort Lauderdale region of Florida are at risk in a Category 2 hurricane. 72.4% of roads in this region are also at risk of a flood, leaving citizens unable to drive to a hospital, or even call an ambulance in a dire situation (Gast et al.). This data was gathered from a model that minimized the chance of a Category 2 storm; although a Category 2 hurricane is very dangerous, it is not even close to the worst a storm can get ("categories" are based on the Saffir-Simpson Hurricane Wind Scale, a 1 to 5 rating in terms of potential property damage, according to the National Hurricane Center).

These statistics are based on past disruptions due to storms in these areas. However, as hurricanes become more dangerous, the number of incapacitated hospitals and beds at risk will increase as well. The researchers found that a rise in sea level of just 0.82 meters caused by climate change would introduce hospitals in six cities that would be unaffected otherwise to potential flooding and closure. In seven cities already at risk, the same increase in sea level would put 50% more beds at risk (Gast et al.). Research has already shown that storms are getting more dangerous now; it is not an issue that can be left for later generations to be concerned about.

When local hospitals close, people who cannot afford to travel to other hospitals or to cover the costs of medevac helicopters or ambulances are left with no escape route. Middle-class families with cars can quickly arrive at hospitals after injuries occur and occupy the limited number of beds available or pay the fee to be transported if road closures occur. Medical resources that require a power source in hospitals may be limited due to the storm and failing generators; often hospitals prioritize people with health insurance more than those without. If a poor family comes in with injuries that require certain scans or equipment that need a power source, they may be refused or pushed off until power is restored to the building.

Further, in coastal regions often hit by storms, there are areas where the land is less likely to be severely affected by a storm. Usually, this land is at a higher elevation and populated by middle- and upper-class families. Homes closer to sea level are much more likely to be flooded and stay flooded until action is taken, whereas those higher up tend to be safer from floods in many storms. On top of this, many of the homes that are closer to the riskiest regions of a striking storm are built with foundations made of weaker materials and less effective structures because it is cheaper. This results in the structure of the home being considerably more susceptible to the strong winds and debris of a storm, as opposed to just the windows being blown out. Flood insurance is much more crucial to have in homes like these. However, it is expensive (around $700 a year), and the people buying and living in these homes with cheaper, weak foundations are less likely to have the ability to invest in it (Milligan). Poor people living in coastal regions off the Atlantic have homes in the most dangerous places if a storm were to hit, built with weaker foundations that will collapse easier than wealthier families' homes, with the inability to afford protection of their belongings when a storm destroys their home, all events that will become inevitable as the Atlantic Ocean becomes more and more unstable due to climate change.

As stated earlier, this is not just an issue on the American Atlantic Coast. Worldwide, poor communities living in areas susceptible to storms are affected by climate change and global warming. In August 2005, Hurricane Katrina touched down in New Orleans off the Gulf Coast, a city just feet above sea level. The Category 3 storm left eighty percent of the city flooded, with well over 100,000 homes and 20,000 businesses destroyed, in addition to the collapse of most schools, fire, and police stations. Almost a fifth of the households below the poverty line in New Orleans did not own a vehicle, providing families with no ability to escape the impending storm before or seek the medicine they needed after. Those who survived and looked for shelters in Louisiana after the storm had to live in other states because of the massive influx of people checking into in-state shelters (Milligan). Since 2005, poverty rates nationwide have increased, leaving more and more people at risk of being victim to storms equivalent to, or worse, than Katrina.

In India, monsoon season results in the deaths of thousands of both homeless and poor and housed people. During August 2018, for example, over 50,000 people were left homeless by monsoon flooding, with nowhere to go: "Homeless shelters often close during the summer months, leaving many to endure the hazardous weather conditions" (Gardner). The combination of the amount of precipitation and the dangerously high temperatures affects the poorest people the most.

Following Tropical Cyclone Idai that struck impoverished countries such as Zimbabwe and Mozambique in March 2019, the UN urged people to recognize the "vulnerability of many low-lying cities and towns to sea-level rise as the impact of climate change continues to influence and disrupt normal weather patterns." In just one city in Mozambique, over 1,500 people were injured due to the storm. They also brought to attention how a setback this large leaves countries affected in even deeper poverty (*United Nations*). Just as the families whose homes were less prepared for a hurricane often do not have the resources to build a new life for themselves, entire countries affected by severe storms can be left with crumbling economies and a lack of morale and resources to rebuild. When most of the schools and medical facilities in a small country are destroyed, the future of the country is also affected. People living in these areas have even fewer resources to escape poverty.

The decline of the environment is not just affecting flora and fauna as the media may make it seem; more times than not, the only articles pushed by news sources are about declining species of plants and animals. People often who cannot afford protection from the forces of nature face the effects of climate change firsthand but receive little news coverage because they are less marketable than the pitying appearance of an endangered animal. When humans are left out of the discussion, those in authority to make or propose change may not care enough about climate change to do so. It is the responsibility of those privileged enough to not have their lives ruined by natural disasters to provide a voice to those in need and propose solutions. There are many layers to this issue as laid out above, and tackling any of them has the potential to save many lives of people cast aside from climate discussions. Even if someone does not believe the increasing danger of hurricanes is caused by human action, the preservation of life should always be a priority, nationally and internationally.

Works Cited

Balaguru, Karthik, et al. "Increasing Hurricane Intensification Rate near the US Atlantic Coast." *Geophysical Research Letters*, vol. 49, no. 20, 28 Oct. 2022. *Web of Science,* https://doi.org/10.1029/2022gl099793. Accessed 20 Feb. 2023.

"'Break the Cycle' of Disaster-Response-Recovery, Urges Top UN Official, as Death Toll Mounts from Cyclone Idai." *United Nations,* United Nations, 18 Mar. 2019, https://news.un.org/en/story/2019/03/1034881.

Gardner, Sophia. "Homelessness during India's Rainy Season." *The Borgen Project*, The Borgen Project, 20 Oct. 2020, https://borgenproject.org/homelessness-during-indias-rainy-season/.

Krause, Eleanor, and Richard V. Reeves. "Hurricanes Hit the Poor the Hardest." *Brookings*, The Brookings Institution, 9 Mar. 2022, https://www.brookings.edu/blog/social-mobility-memos/2017/09/18/hurricanes-hit-the-poor-the-hardest/.

Milligan, Susan. "The Forecast for Recovery." *U.S. News*, U.S. News & World Report L.P., 21 Sept. 2018, https://www.usnews.com/news/the-report/articles/2018-09-21/hurricanes-hit-everyone-but-the-poor-have-the-hardest-time-recovering.

Rivlin, Gary. "White New Orleans Has Recovered from Hurricane Katrina. Black New Orleans Has Not." *Talk Poverty,* Center for American Progress, 29 Aug. 2016, https://talkpoverty.org/2016/08/29/white-new-orleans-recovered-hurricane-katrina-black-new-orleans-not/.

"Saffir-Simpson Hurricane Wind Scale." *National Hurricane Center and Central Pacific Hurricane Center,* National Oceanic and Atmosphere Administration, https://www.nhc.noaa.gov/aboutsshws.php#:~:text=The%20Saffir%2DSimpson%20Hurricane%20Wind,Scale%20estimates%20potential%20property%20damage.

Tarabochia-Gast, A. T., et al. "Flood Risk to Hospitals on the United States Atlantic and Gulf Coasts from Hurricanes and Sea Level Rise." *GeoHealth*, vol. 6, no. 10, Oct. 2022. Web of Science, https://doi.org/10.1029/2022gh000651. Accessed 20 Feb. 2023.

Withers, Paul. "The Labrador Sea Keeps the World's Oceans Alive. Scientists Are Now Closer to Understanding How." *CBCnews,* CBC/Radio Canada, 6 Feb. 2022, https://www.cbc.ca/news/canada/nova-scotia/labrador-sea-research-oxygen-transfer-world-oceans-1.6340451.

Drexel Publishing Group

Creative Writing

Introduction

The following creative works were selected by faculty judges from student submissions (of creative nonfiction, fiction, humor, and poetry) to the Drexel Publishing Group Creative Writing Contest. There were many strong entries in all categories. The pieces in this section engage with a wide range of topics, including parents, illness, heartbreak, dreams, and the challenges of being an adult. They are thoughtful, introspective, and brave. These student writers demonstrate insight, humor, and a profound understanding of our current times.

—*The Editors*

Michael Emmert
Paternity Leave

I felt for his car keys underneath my pillow, gripping them as I listened to his footsteps creak in the next room. I felt his weight shift from board to board through the old house and finally onto the bed. Slipping out from under my covers, I released the keys and crept my way to the bedroom door. My ears followed the noise that came from the next room: a single monotone voice droning on. I carefully stepped out of the room and gripped the railing in the hallway to distribute my weight. From the next room over, a dim peach fuzz glow peeked through the door's cracks where my father was now staying. I peered into the room. The man was laying on the bed, eyes fixed on the ceiling and sharing anecdotes with some white space.

He spoke softly. "I don't really remember Jenny."

"Yeah, I know we worked together, but it was in different buildings."

"She had a nice ass," he laughed, his voice starting to boom.

"You guys joke way too much. I can't handle it."

"But you know I would never do that to Cheryl."

In the hallway I slumped down onto the hardwood floor. I wept as I listened to him talk on about my mother, his job, lovers, and some childhood stories. I had never heard him talk this much before, nor had I ever learned so much about him. Tracing the wood grain with my fingers, I stayed listening to his voice. It was so lively compared to a couple months prior. He spoke for hours. I found out who he was besides my father: an avid Foo Fighters fan; a gambler; a baseball enthusiast. I wondered if this was who he was under the shy, reserved composure he had since my childhood.

His voice reverberated around the room. "I can't do that anymore."

"Gamble? With what money?"

"I don't know guys?" The room sat empty besides his voice filling each crevice.

"They want me to take it."

"I think they just care about me. I don't know. You know how she can be."

"My son is fine with it, I don't think he understands, he just worries."

"You're right, it could be anything. I won't."

I heard a movement from the bed. I leapt up and slid back into my bedroom, shutting the door softly behind me. Once in bed, I listened to stomping down the hall and into the bathroom. The flick of the light switch. The hum of the fan. A murmur of my father's voice still talking. This time it felt muffled, as if he was trying to keep himself from speaking. He stifled his laughs and ran the water in the sink, his voice raised a bit as the water splashed. I laid in the dark, staring at the ceiling, hoping tomorrow would be quieter.

Over the next few weeks, the chatter would continue. I wondered who my father spoke with and what they looked like, if they had appearances at all. I imagined three people, a woman with red hair and two tall sporty men. They reminded me of old friends of his I saw in a photograph once. When I had the courage to ask, he simply told me that he wasn't speaking with anyone, he was rehearsing conversations. I accepted this as a poor attempt to get me to think he was healthy. I watched him through a mania in which he transformed into someone unrecognizable and rambunctious. Never had I seen him strive to work out, clean, eat healthy, or find hobbies. I didn't mind this aspect of his condition at the time, I was happy he was less depressive than who he was before. Yet this still came at a cost; while he was trying to better himself, he was still a man that spoke with empty space, and he was like a reckless kid in this state.

In our nightly routine, I slipped my father his little orange pill and watched as his throat gulped when he took it. I thanked him and checked off "Tuesday night" on the medication chart we kept next to the pill box. He marched upstairs on his way to bed, stuttering under his breath. I ensured his pills were set up for the week and followed him. Upstairs I listened to him run the water from the bathroom sink. As I got closer to the door, I heard a muffled gagging and the splashing of water from inside.

I called through the door, "Hey, what are you doing? Are you okay?"

"I am brushing my teeth; don't come in," he yelled back at me.

Ignoring this, I forced the door open. The sterile fluorescent white light shined down onto my father, his hand gripping the dull yellow tile on the wall. Blooms of orange pigment lined the bowl of the sink, they streaked like watercolor as they cascaded down the drain. An orange foam dribbled from his lips and down onto the collar of his shirt as if he was a toddler. Saliva coated the surrounding of his lips and he hurried to wipe it with a cloth. He looked primal. Against a bloodshot sclera, his blue eyes shot through me: dilated, veiny, and fearful. Staring at me, his eyes grew wet and heavy, like a child who had just done something wrong. I looked back, relinquishing. "Alright sorry, I was just making sure you were okay." I shut the door, heading back to my bedroom, wondering how to care for a stranger.

Sharon Sohmen

Enough

It was 11 P.M. on an uncharacteristically chilly night in April when my father stopped our car in front of the ER doors in my hometown. I stepped out and walked through the sliding doors to get one of the wheelchairs from inside. *Unlock, push, accelerate to make it over the bump on the pavement.* These ER trips had become more or less a regular occurrence for us since my mother's diagnosis in December.

She had stage 3 pancreatic cancer. Her chemo regimen had been so hard on her body she was unable to eat solid food for months. Every biweekly chemo session was followed by extreme fatigue that was further worsened by her lack of appetite. The neuropathy—which caused numbness and weakness in her hands and feet—became exacerbated by the arrival of the cold winter months, causing her pain when she held anything. She began to lose her hair, starting with hair on her head, followed by her eyebrows and eyelashes. The doctors seemed to understand all of these. But one particularly mysterious byproduct of her treatment was the painful swelling it caused in her feet. Since she began this chemo regimen, they began to balloon and redden, and eventually, my mother needed help to walk even to the bathroom. Every time this mysterious side-effect flared up and became unbearable, we prepared for a visit to the ER. So, the night my mother said her right eye's vision was half blocked by something that looked like a black film, we knew what to do: I packed my tote bag, and we left for the ER.

Accelerate up the slight incline and back over the bump. I wheeled my mother into the ER. Soon after, I was told I could accompany her to one of the curtained rooms down the hallway, where a doctor met us and determined that my mother had a detached retina, a medical emergency. If she did not undergo surgery immediately, she risked completely losing her right eye's vision—luckily, a world-renowned eye hospital where this procedure could be done was close by, in downtown Philadelphia. The ER arranged for medical transportation to take my mother to the eye hospital where she could be ready to promptly begin the surgery.

So, the stretcher came to take her away. I looked at my mother who tried to maintain her lively expression in her exhausted state, and in that unsettlingly pristine hallway at 4 A.M. on that cold April morning, time seemed so finite, and life, so precious. And for the first time since the diagnosis, I cried in front of her.

Looking back, the surgery she would undergo to restore her right eye's sight was not objectively life threatening, but in that moment, I could not see past my fear of this extreme situation. Maybe what broke the dam I had maintained for so long was the look in my mother's eyes anticipating another blow to her already depleted health, or maybe it was a buildup of emotions from the preceding five months. Maybe it was everything all at once.

As I looked at my mother on that stretcher, for what I thought, at 4 A.M., could be the very last time, my lips quivered and my heart sank. *So weak. You had to do one thing.* She had always felt our pain as her own. She began to cry as well, saying in our native language, *"Nuvu edustay, nenu bharinchalenu"*—"If you cry, I cannot bear it." I knew that was true, and the guilt washed over me. All this time, I held myself to one standard of strength above all else: not letting my mother see my tears. And I failed.

The paramedics began to strap her up in preparation for the bumpy ride downtown in the ambulance, and my disappointment morphed into fear. I had to say "bye" to her, for what I believed could be the last time before this unfamiliar surgery at an unfamiliar hospital. My mind raced as I wondered how to fit a lifetime of love—staying up until early morning to bring me coffee as I crammed for a test, letting me hate her for a moment so I could grow into the person she knew I could be, sacrificing her own happiness for mine in a heartbeat—into a single goodbye. All I could say was, "I love you, Mummy." And that statement, though the truest thing I know, was painfully insufficient.

But it was okay. Because I knew with all my heart, that she knew. She knew what I felt, and what I meant, because she had spent every fiber of her being for the past 20 years loving my sister and me. Even though in my mind at that moment, I had failed to be strong for her, and let my weakness cause her pain, I knew she did not see the weakness I had already condemned myself for. And that was enough. Throughout my life, no matter how many times I felt deficient and inadequate, love—from my mother, sister, father, and my God—made me enough. And though I didn't know what lay ahead, I knew in my heart that it would be okay. I knew that we would be okay.

Megan Kline

The Elephant

Spiritual: relating to or affecting the human spirit or soul, as opposed to material or physical things.

I would consider myself a spiritual person. Not the kind that goes to a church or prays every night, but the kind that believes things have a deeper meaning. I would always believe in superstitions, whether they are broken mirrors or open umbrellas inside. I also believe in the different meanings of crystals and statues. I believe that sometimes things have a deeper meaning, even if they are something we can't directly see. Except at this moment, I did see it.

I was fifteen at the time, the age when if you wanted to go somewhere, you had to walk because you couldn't drive just yet. I spent most of my time walking to thrift stores. I liked the idea of buying unique things that might be hard to get anywhere else. It was a cold January day during winter break. I remember feeling as if frost was lining my face while I settled into my usual route to the thrift store. On my way, I came across a house not too far from mine with stuff scattered across the yard and a little sign that read, "Moving out, take whatever." Older, almost vintage stuff without the price? Don't mind if I do! There were vinyls, blankets, and little jewelry boxes that sing when you open them. I walked away with this long brown wooden box, about double the size of a standard iPhone, and these two little elephant statues. The elephants were the big find of the day. They stood about two inches tall and were completely white. They felt like glass, giving them a nice shine. They lacked pupils in their eyes, but I thought a little paint would fix that. I was familiar with the spiritual idea of elephants in different cultures, which is why I was so attracted to them. I remember reading about the significance of their trunks; when it is up, it represents good luck, and when it is angled down, it represents misfortune. These statues had theirs up, so I thought it was perfect. The trunk had a small diameter, which would fit a ring perfectly, bringing a little luck.

I walked back to my house content with all my finds for the day, but mostly because I wanted to give one of the elephant statues to my mom. My mom is picky about her jewelry, especially her wedding ring. I would be too if mine was as extravagant as hers. She has two rings, one that she wears most of the time and the other that she wears to work. So, I thought this would be a perfect place to put her fancy ring while she's at work since luck would keep it from getting lost.

I stood in the living room with my hand raised dramatically, as if I were in school waiting for her to give me attention. I would do this often, so she was automatically unfazed by my theatrical gesture.

"What?" she asked as she paused her show on the TV.

"I brought you a gift home," I replied as I was eagerly digging into my pocket. "It's a little figure for your ring. It's like a display kind of."

I handed it to her, watching her examine the statue. I assumed she was looking for a price tag that she would never find.

"It's pretty. Did you get it from the store?" She didn't seem as excited as I was.

"No, I got it from a house that had some random belongings across their yard. It's good luck, you know, the statue." She didn't seem convinced, so I rambled on. "Remember in Epcot, in Disney, there were elephant statues in China with other spiritual objects around them, some of their cultures believe the elephant to be a spiritual animal, and the trunks have different meanings..." I continued. I began to trail off as she gave me a doubtful look. She was never much of a spiritual person, at least from what I had seen before the moment. At the same moment, I saw the deeper meaning of that elephant.

At the beginning of February, a few weeks after my trip to the free yard sale, I got a text from my dad. He explained the neighbors called and told him the house was emitting smoke. He was not the best at explaining the situation, just questioning whether my brother and I left a lit candle in our rooms. It wasn't until after the back and forth of questions that my dad confirmed my house caught fire. The house was burning for three hours before anyone was aware of it, until some strangers on the main road saw the smoke and pulled into our neighborhood to call the fire department. Without them, the house would have been completely gone. No one in my family was near; I was at school, my dad was out of state, and my mom was at work.

My sister got there first, running over a mile from her house to ours so that someone was there while waiting for my mom. She informed us the fire focused on the left side of my house the most. My parents' room. The room where my mom keeps her jewelry was at the heart of the fire. The journey to even get to my house dragged on for hours. The roads around my house were blocked, making it over a mile walk in the cold. I had many thoughts racing through my mind during that walk, most regarding my cat, who might not be alive when I saw her. Time dragged on as the fire department was doing their walkthrough, seeing what was stable and what was not before we were finally allowed in the house. My mom was the only one allowed in, but my brother, sister, and I followed her anyway. We all wanted to see the damage done to our home, and find our cat that was stuck in the destruction, proud to say she was alright. After we found her and everything, there were a few things we each wanted to look for most; and for my mom, it was her ring.

My parents' room was on the fourth floor, but at that moment, it was on the second floor. The entire fourth floor was on the second floor, to be exact. It was as if it had never existed in the first place. We all stood in the living room looking up at what should have been the ceiling but was the rainy sky. Due to the lack of stability, we were not allowed to go above the second floor. My room was on the third floor, so I spent the rest of the time wondering what my room looked like. I wanted to know if my walls were still white or if my clothes were still clean, or if my room was even still my room. We didn't have anywhere to go, so we had to wait for my dad to get a plane and make his way to us. We reluctantly chose to pass the time by rummaging through the second-floor debris as much as we could. Most of the rummaging was spent seeing if my mom's ring managed to fall onto the second floor with everything else. Not a single word was spoken during the search. None of us even mentioned exactly what we were looking for, but somehow all of us knew. The moments of silence dragged on, only hearing the little thuds of rubble from getting tossed around the floor. The only words spoken were by my brother.

"Maybe if we could get Nick's metal detector it would be a lot less of a mess." We all knew he didn't mean it; he was the sarcastic one out of all of us.

We did manage to get a little chuckle out of my mom, but with more of a sigh mixed in. I started to lift the office chair that was now displayed on the dining room table, and there it was, there was the ring under a piece of ceiling. The ring was there, but so was the elephant. The elephant was still in perfect shape and didn't even look dull from ash and smoke. What a lucky, lucky statue. My mom was relieved but hid her emotions well; not even a wrinkle of relief showed. She held the ring in her hand for a few moments before making me run out to the car. I would have thought she would slip it on, but I guess having it lost in a fire for a few hours was all she could handle. I know she was happy to have it, even if she didn't let her face show it.

Now I may not feel the spirit levels of the elephant the way other cultures do, but I have my meaning. Instead of luck, I see it as a feeling of safety. It brought a little bit of comfort to this traumatic experience, and at the time, comfort was the only emotion I was able to process full-heartedly. She still makes those faces at me whenever I bring home my other statues or rocks, but she has that elephant right next to her bedside, still holding onto the ring.

First Place—Fiction

Wren Francis

Blue Roses

"Blue roses? Who the hell buys blue roses? They do know they're dyed, right?"

We are at the Farmer's Market, our favorite place to go, and I am not paying attention because I am 27 days late.

"Hmm? Oh, yeah. Weird." I pick at the skin on my finger. I know I should tell you. I know what you'll say. You'll tell me, *Baby, it's probably nothing. Aren't you on the pill anyway?* and I will smile and nod and go back to my apartment and look in the hallway mirror and pull my shirt up to check if there's been a change since the morning.

You're still talking about the damn roses, your hands flying through the air as you grin, your hair falling in your eyes just so and I think, *God, I've really done it now, haven't I?*

***

We walk back to your place. You didn't buy the blue roses, but put them back and winked at me, as though it was our little secret that you had wanted to. I am calculating the chances with each step. *Okay, maybe I missed a pill? Step. But even if I missed one, I should still have a buildup of the chemicals in my system, right? Step. I have to check the pack when I get home. Step.* I've googled the chances of it happening over twenty times today alone. It's .3%. I know this. But I keep thinking that maybe if I look it up again, I'll find a source that says there's no chance.

I almost walk right past your door, and you look at me sideways as we head in.

"You okay?" I nod, rub my eyes like I'm tired (I am the opposite of tired), and yawn.

"Just sleepy. All that sunshine really wears me out. Do you mind if I head upstairs and take a nap?" You kiss the top of my head as an answer, turn, and walk into the kitchen. Quietly, I hurry up the steps, and when I'm at the top, I check the room on the left, where your roommate Steve sleeps. He's not there. *Shit.* I can hear you in the kitchen, humming to yourself as the water runs, and my heart aches. You want to be a father so badly. We've talked about it before, on nights where the two of us have had a couple glasses of wine and we're curled on the couch and you say *God, I can't wait to have a family with you.*

I taste bile in my mouth. I'm 27 days late and we haven't had sex in over three months.

***

After my "nap" (where I didn't sleep but stared at the ceiling for hours), I head out.

The man at the CVS down the street gives me a concerned look when I slide the test onto the counter, and for a second, I want to tell him. I want to explain myself to a complete stranger. But I bite my tongue, pay in cash and tuck the test into the back of my jeans. It would make me feel a bit better if there was any chance in hell of this baby belonging to you. But there's just no way.

I started to think that maybe you were interested in other people. Every time we'd go out, I would watch you and monitor how you reacted to girls out in public. But you never seemed into them, so I ruled that out. My other option was that school was getting hectic. Maybe you were so busy with classes that you couldn't focus on having sex right now. But then one month blended into two, and then three, and we still didn't talk about it. We haven't talked about it. We just pass each other, exchange our proper pleasantries and the occasional kiss, but it's never anything more than that. And I wanted more than that. We used to have more than that.

It was so easy. Part of me thinks I did it to get back at you, to say a big fuck you and just do it once, just so I could say that I did. You were away at a crew meet. I came by the apartment on my way home, and as I knocked, I wasn't sure I wanted anyone to answer. After a minute, Steve opened the front door, beer in hand.

"Hey, Sam. You know he's at a meet, right?"

"Yeah, yeah. I just—I wanted to see you." He raised an eyebrow. "I mean I, I—can I come in?" The door swung wide.

***

We spent the night on the couch, chatting over a couple more beers. He's cute if you look at him in the right light, but he isn't anything like you. You're tall, strong and so sweet you could rot cavities into your own teeth with the force of your smile. Steve isn't like that. He's lanky, and sharp-tongued, always quick with a joke or a witty retort. It wasn't that I wanted him. I wanted somebody, and he was there.

It started with a gentle nudge to the shoulder. We were laughing, and he leaned in and bumped my shoulder against his. I blushed, and he pulled back, looking down into his lap. I mustered up all the anger I had coursing through my veins, all the confusion and the hurt and the want, and I took his chin in my hand.

"It's okay. This is okay."

I leaned in first. His mouth isn't like yours, it's rougher and smaller, and he kisses with his teeth first. But all I wanted were his hands on me, so I reached out and put them there. He hesitated only slightly, then started feeling around. His hands were under my shirt, and I was gasping, and his mouth was on my neck and then we were standing, my legs wrapped around his waist as he carried me upstairs.

We went to his bedroom, and when he reached to turn on the light, I stopped him.

"No, just us and the dark. It's better that way." Truly, I didn't want to see the monster I'd become. We fumbled with our clothes, and as he was pulling his jeans off, I said, "Do you use condoms?"

"No, it feels nicer without them." I didn't care. I was on the pill anyway. And it would be an even bigger "fuck you" to you if he fucked me raw.

***

Afterwards, he rolled out of bed and tugged his jeans on. I felt disgusting. The guilt came in as soon as the high faded, and I knew I had done something irreversible.

"I'm gonna go down the street and buy more beers. You want anything?" I shook my head, but in the dark Steve couldn't see it anyway. He took my silence as an answer, and without saying another word, walked out of the room. I listened to him take the stairs two at a time and heard the clunk of the front door being shut, and that's when I let the tears come. *How could I have done this to you?* You, the man I'd been dating for three years, how could I have just done this to you?

I pulled myself out of the bed, still crying, and put my clothes back on. I wanted to be gone before he came back. I walked down your stairs and out your front door, knowing in my soul that I had broken us.

***

I am standing with the test in my hand, watching for lines to appear. One line. All I need is one line and I'm home free. I'd never have to think about this again.

I put the test face down on the sink and set a timer on my phone

What will my parents say? Do I tell you? What would I tell you? "Hey, we haven't had sex in months, but surprise! I'm pregnant!" Yeah, that would go over so well. I run my hands through my hair and stare at the stick. I want to flip it over, but at the same time I'm not ready to see. I can't see. This can't be real. *This can't be happening.*

My phone's timer starts ringing, making me jump. When I shut it off, the silence feels heavy. My heart is racing. I can hear it in my ears. I feel like I'm going to pass out. Squeezing my eyes shut, I grab the test, and turn it over in my hands. I force myself to look down, and— slowly—I open my eyes.

Blinking up at me are two lines.

***

I check it again. Two lines. The test falls from my fingers and hits the tile floor. *I'm pregnant. I'm in the .3%. How is this happening?* I stoop and pick the test up off the ground with shaking fingers. Two lines. My breathing picks up. *I'm pregnant. Oh my god I'm pregnant.* I put my hands in my hair and tug, trying to calm myself down. I need to go home. I need to get out of your apartment. I need to leave.

I wrench the bathroom door open and grab my purse from your dresser, tossing the test and its box into it. I take a panicked look around your room and think, *oh God I'm so fucked. I'm so fucked.*

***

Three days after the test, I start to bleed. I am at your apartment when I notice it, a bright red smear on the toilet paper and I think *it's only a little, and the blogs I've been reading say that's normal,* but as the day wears on it gets heavier. I wrap toilet paper around my underwear as a makeshift pad, but by lunch, I am in so much pain I can't stand straight. You take my hand and help me up the stairs, asking me every step if there's anything you can do. I don't tell you. I still don't tell you. I just keep saying, "It must've been something I ate." We walk past Steve's room, and he's there, headphones on and knee deep in a game. I want to scream at him. I want to beat him with my fists and say, *look, look what you've done to me you stupid bastard. You just had to be a proud sonofabitch and not wear a condom, didn't you! Fuck you!*

You help me to the bathroom, and I get you to leave by saying I don't want you to see me so sick. You make a small noise of protest, but you walk away. I manage to get myself onto the toilet and I curl forwards, pressing my hands against my stomach. *Is this hell? Am I in hell?*

***

When it's all over, I take the stairs slowly, holding onto the banister. I can hear the TV. *Did I just lose a baby?*

As I turn the corner into the hallway, you come out of the kitchen holding a vase.

"Baby, I thought this might cheer you up! See, blue roses, like that day at the Farmer's Market?" My cheeks heat up. Here you are, in all your goofy, wonderful glory, and you have no idea. You don't know what I've done, what's happened, what's changed me. But I smile and take your hand as you begin to tell me about your latest regatta. A distant part of myself feels relieved, but the majority of me feels like I just ran a marathon and a triathlon in the same day.

As we curl up on the couch, you put your arm around me and I press my ear against your chest, hearing your heartbeat. *I'll never hear its heartbeat.*

"Hey, I love you so much, you know that, right? Nothing is ever going to change that." I nod. My lip trembles.

I'll never hear its heartbeat.

Lillian Fenzil
Till the End of the Line

"Pass the…" Nessa put the pin cushion in my hand before I could finish the sentence. Three months trapped with another person helps you learn their routines. COVID hadn't been kind to anyone, especially to students trapped in an apartment with someone they met a year before. I stab the extra blue quilting pin in the red cushion. "Thanks."

She hovers over the couch, where I continue stitching, then plops down next to me to focus on the show we were streaming, *What We Do In the Shadows*. "Best show ever; best representation of vampires yet."

I barely look up from the needle. We've watched a lot of crappy vampire shows in the past few weeks. "What? Fictional beings need representation?"

"Duh. They're so cool!"

Rolling my eyes, I didn't bother starting an argument. My hand continues pulling the thread between the layers of fabric and batting, and for a moment, I zone out. It's been happening a lot more lately—since I stopped taking my medication two months ago. When quarantine began, I noticed a huge weight off my shoulders. No deadlines, no social interaction, no expectations. I could sit, watch TV, and craft all day. My mental health improved drastically, so the meds seemed pointless. Nessa agreed. A sharp pain bloomed on my index finger, bringing me back to the present. The needle was inserted deep, blood trickling around the entrance point. "Oh."

Nessa must have realized before me as she went to grab band-aids and cleaning tools. I had to look away as she pulled the needle smoothly out and began patching it up.

"All set," she mumbled, and when I looked back at her, she had the needle bit between her teeth. She pulled it out and explained, "Didn't want to get any of the surfaces dirty. We should probably go to bed, so you don't stab yourself again."

I opened my phone, 5:57 am. "Probably a good idea."

Our sleep schedule was messed up by the third night of quarantine. Watching movies till midnight the first night led to watching movies till two the second, and so on. At this point, we've decided to join the creatures on screen and be nocturnal.

"Wouldn't dare being up when the sun rises," we laughed off.

***

Time continued to inch by in a blink, and our routine continued. Quilt, watch *Twilight*, cook, watch *Buffy the Vampire Slayer*. At one point, my mom called. Nessa said to not bother, so I let it ring to voicemail. By the time July hit,

I had multiple missed calls from my mom, a new quilt, and a perfected recipe of nectarine upside down cake.

Nessa was out this morning...evening? It was ten o'clock at night? Either way, she was picking up Chinese takeout for later in the night. I always thought it was kind. Nessa was a picky eater and refused most foods I offered, but she was always willing to go out and grab whatever garlicky concoction I wanted.

As soon as she walked out the door, my phone rang. Buzzing against the counter, I could see the word, "MOM," flashing across the screen. Nessa wasn't here to stop me, and I did miss my mom. It rang three times before I yanked the phone to my ear.

"Mom?" I didn't know what else to say.

"Darling? Why haven't you picked up your phone? I was one missed call from traveling across the country in a pandemic to see you." Her voice was firm, yet warm. It felt like home—a warm embrace, the smell of banana bread, my bed that I could just melt into—tears began forming in my eyes as she continued, "I was worried."

Those three words caused me to break into tears. "I'm sorry, mom," I try to say through sobs.

"It's alright. It's been a hard few months. I just want to make sure you are okay. You were having a hard time last we spoke."

I tried to recall the last time we talked, but the door interrupted my thought process. Nessa entered looking grim.

"Hi, everything go well?"

My mom responded instead with a concerned tone. "Who are you talking to?"

"Oh. Nessa just walked through the door with some food. She's been making sure I eat," but instead of chiming in to say hi, she reached for my phone.

I barely heard my mom's response, "Honey, we went to Nessa's funeral in early March, remember? Have you been taking your—"

"I told you not to bother," Nessa says to me as she hangs up. "I'm the only friend you need."

Cassandra Stathis
A God's Losing Game

This story is about how a god stepped and tripped over his own toes and lost to a mortal. I was born to King Priam and Queen Hecuba, making me the Princess of Troy. My childhood years were that of a shitty princess life, sitting in silence contemplating nothing because girls don't think or whatever those men say. What a waste of time. However, as I grew, I was allowed to have my own hobbies. On a day the same as any other, most importantly minding my business, I was walking in my personal garden tending to my vegetation, when all of a sudden, Apollo appeared, rudely crushing my campanulas. *Putanas yos.* No seriously, you hear about these kinds of stories all the time. They show up and do whatever, I really have no idea why. Don't they have jobs to do? No wonder the sun doesn't set at the same time every day and our crops have a shit time growing. He is too busy getting into everyone's pants.

"Kassandra, Princess of Troy, daughter of Ki..."

You already know.

He should really move.

"Whatever it is you're trying to do, could you please for the love of all the gods, get off my flowers?"

He stays where he is. Apollo continues.

"Do you know who I am? Princess of Troy, daughter of..."

Is this guy serious? Let's see: die by natural causes or be smitten to death by a god. Eh, truly, either outcome is fine. I cut him off again.

"I very much do know who you are, considering I'm a priestess for you. And this might surprise you, but I also know who I am, so you don't need to keep repeating your monologue. What exactly do you want?"

"I am Apollo, god of the sun, god of music, god of poetry, god of truth, god of archery, god of..."

Good gods, why would anyone want to brag about listening to gods talk about themselves? Is he still going?

"...of plague, god of healing, and god of light."

"I very much know."

"I couldn't help but take note of your beauty."

What? That's how he makes an entrance to compliment a woman, stepping right onto her poor flowers that are very much dead at this point. I need to get him out of here.

"Listen, I'm flattered, but..."

"I can offer you the gift of prophecy."

Vges éxo, get out! Why? Maybe I can use it to predict the next time a methýstakas tramples my poor babies. Let's speed this up.

"In return for???"

"Your love and possibly your hand in marriage."

Oh no. Is this the part of my life that I'm in right now? I wish I saw this coming, the true curse of being a princess. Ugh, I just want him off my flowers! Just go with it, Kassandra, if you go with it maybe he'll leave faster.

Batting my eyelashes, I spoke. "Oh wow, the Olympian god Apollo, god of the sun, aski-"

"And the god of music, god of poetry, god of tru..."

"Asking for my love in return! Of being blessed with the gift of prophecy?!" I continued before he could say another worthless word, "How could I say no?"

"Perfect!"

The silence grew.

"Now why don't we head to the local inn, it's just down the road, they have a really good tavern," Apollo said while trying to grab my hand.

"Wait, I was promised a gift?" Ripping my fingers away from his.

"And you have it!"

That was it? Well, that was very anticlimactic. Damn, I really don't want to leave. But hey, maybe it'll be fun doing something I'm not usually allowed to do.

"Maybe we can even get a room and spend some time alone." Apollo's eyebrows wiggle in emphasis.

Get a room????

"Excuse me?" I said beginning to take a few steps backward.

"We're practically husband and wife."

Practically??? Today was the first, and hopefully, the last, time I met him! I always understood how ridiculous it was for mortals to be with gods, but now I get it. It's not us, it's them.

"Yeah right, I don't do that with someone I just met."

"But it's been a whole twenty minutes, we're soulmates."

This guy managed to cut my patience even shorter.

"No, I can't do this, this is absolutely ridiculous. I thought accepting your foolish gift would get you to leave faster but, damn it, was I wrong."

"Foolish?!" Apollo yells, "you want foolish, I'll give you foolishness. Do you know what you just have done?"

I really don't care. And he goes to open his mouth..."Now when you speak your prophecy, you will be seen as a fool. No one shall believe in the things you say."

I quickly jump in, "Then I won't speak it."

His golden sculpted face turns a deep red. *Is this where I die? Finally, a way out of this.*

"...That's not how it works!" He continues, "you will be seen as untrustworthy to friends, family, everyone! Your words will become worthless."

Oh! Is he done with his little tantrum?

"...Okay"

He begins to pull out his bow and arrow. When I'm expecting death, I get peace instead. He's gone. Did I just experience a long-term married life in a forty-minute time span? His biggest mistake was not listening to me in the first place. At least I can fix my campanulas. Poor babies.

I told my father, my brother Hector, even spoke to that *malakas—a "nice" way of calling someone a donkey—*of a god Apollo. Troy was going to fall in a way that they would never expect. A giant horse that held Greek soldiers in its stomach. They told me I was a foolish girl, I was wrong, and it was a stupid way to invade Troy. Ho boy. They should be so grateful I went out of my way to tell them. But that's okay, I won't be the one who looks foolish. Most of the city is in fear and panic is on the rise. Worrying about their sons going to war, worrying about food supply, and keeping their personal belongings close. But for me, I grabbed my things and left. I still watched from a distance. Apollo thinks he won over me, but I'm not the one about to lose my city. I prefer to keep to myself anyways. I really only need my gift to make sure no *methýstakas* steps on my campanulas.

First Place—Poetry

Matthew D'Esposito
I Don't Think About My Dreams

I don't think about my dreams

they come to me—

like faded photographs,

mesmerized with lines and creases

an unconscious album

old, but new.

I don't think about my dreams

they try me out

a dirty film reel

collecting heat as it spins

from blood-streaked cave paintings to

Madame X, back again to hairy armpits

forest fires, pastrami on rye

race horses and genital bins

an apartment complex with a bullet wound

built over a field of knotted tongues

I must salute to a lost friend gone!

I don't think about my dreams

they are me—

stars poured, liquified

one thousand honey masks

glazed over my eyes

I am more deaf than blind,

but blind enough to follow them

into sweet decay.

Wren Francis
Rotten Pickles, Gestures and Love

Those pickles in the fridge back home

are probably bad by now —

I haven't been there

in going on four years.

I left everything in that rotting house

with a rotting husband

and a rotting dream,

every love-lined gesture

a Stage Kiss in his eyes

and the world in mine.

I always wanted to be loved,

a love like the movies,

and maybe that just wasn't meant for me.

God knows I'm dog-tired,

worn so thin,

I have holes at the elbows of the old jacket you gave me,

and my toes poke through my socks.

The last time we danced to the Beatles,

I watched the love die on your face

as I stupidly asked you if we should try for kids.

I knew you hated children,

so wound up in your past that you couldn't see

five feet into a better future.

But I thought maybe you loved me more

and that I could change your mind.

Funny. I should have known better.

My grandad warned me to

read the skies for storms,

new car smell deep in my bones

as I chased the lightning out west,

as I far as I could get

away from the Sky Rocket at the Fair

off the Long Island Sound

where we met when we were just thirteen.

I still check up on Your Facebook Timeline,

to see the dogs,

to see you.

I wonder if they miss my smell.

I wonder if you miss anything about me.

Probably not,

but it's a nice thought.

Note: This prompt was taken from Poems for the Writing: Prompts for Poets (Second Edition). Fox, V., & Levin, L. (2021).

Phrases to be Used:

New car smell	Chairs not fastened
Dog-tired	Stage Kiss
Your Facebook Timeline	A rabbit's fur
Those pickles in the fridge	The ants at the picnic
Read the skies for storms	The Sky Rocket at the Fair
It's what we call a triple threat	The last time we danced to the Beatles

Matthew D'Esposito
Le Violin d'Ingres

I can't take my eyes off Man Ray's *Le Violin d'Ingres*.

Black-and-white,

twelve by eight inches, the woman is nude

facing forward or away like a chess piece

on a board made of pinched shadows.

Is she the queen or a pawn?

Her shapeless back does not twitch

despite being a kind of musician:

a bone instrument with little face and no arms,

hair contained in dispossessed beauty,

legs wrapped in something resembling

the mouth of a curtain.

Does she know it's swallowing

her with those silk teeth?

Working its way up to the only voice

she has, carved into her back.

I wonder if you put your hands

through her hollow body you can hear

her spine play and heart thump,

but is she made of flesh or wood?

Does she have veins or strings? Blood or sound?

Is she snapped away in a case when

they are done with her or does she wait to be played

again by the maestro, Man Ray?

Resting his head on her pearl-white thigh as if

it was a pillow, his dreams spilling over

her skin to hide what is there and what is missing,

a kind of death draped over her

as she poses like a modernist Barbie doll before

the eye history is recorded through,

this woman was somehow real

yet a figment of imagination

so crude and absurd

it needed to be photographed, copied

hung up in museums and auctioned

folded and put in pockets

it needed to be considered lust to be art

and I am still left unsure whether she

is a violin or woman or even there at all.

Chris Faunce

Staying Young

Sure, I'll walk into work

with a collared shirt

and use the money to buy a house

and build a family.

But I'll still be a child inside—

riding waves into the sand,

crying when my first and second

hamsters passed away.

I'll still be a child inside,

even as an old man

handing crinkled candy

to a tiny hand, the child blinking

from too much light

reflecting off the wrapper.

Literature Essay

Introduction

The essay in this section is the winner of the Literature Essay Contest. Essays must be submitted by (or nominated by) faculty teaching literature courses. Literature faculty are asked to select essays that demonstrate excellence in writing. These essays explore a variety of literary topics. The editors are pleased to include the winning literature essay in *The 33rd*.

—*The Editors*

Randee Wismer

The Role of Man in Woman's Narrative

Bernadine Evaristo's *Girl, Woman, Other* is a story of female triumph and tribulation. It follows the lives of 11 women and one non-binary person as they make their way in this world, largely without the help of men. The absence of men in the book is extremely apparent, either through the lack of a male role, or the "presence" of a missing father/husband in each of the narratives. The lack of men could not go ignored in my reading of the book, nor could the role of the men that do appear as villains.

An all-women's narrative (much less an 11-women's narrative) is so out of the normal literary sphere, that the absent men stuck out like a sore thumb. Even though I should have been celebrating this collection of women's stories, of women's struggles and their triumphs without the help of men, I was left wondering, *where are the fathers/husbands/men?* The presence of the strong male protagonist is so ingrained in me, that I was searching for it in this book; or looking to see how the book functioned without this "integral" part of each story, the man as hero. My obsession over looking for the men in a story where they don't belong surprised me and even saddened me. But this is exactly why I think I should look into it further. What is the role of man in the woman's narrative? The men in *Girl, Woman, Other* frequently serve as the antagonists (or even, I would go so far as to say, the villains) of the story. By comparing the roles of heroes vs. heroines, identifying when female characters take on male roles, identifying male characters as antagonists, and highlighting the successes of the women in the face of the absent male, I will hopefully be doing some work towards unlearning the man as the hero and show how Evaristo positions man as the antithesis to woman.

In literature, there seem to be classical differences between a hero and a heroine. The heroine is not just a female hero, but has a very different role to play: "the female hero is characterised by sacrifice...who sacrifices her life to uphold patriarchal authority and a higher moral order...the purpose of whose sacrifices is the preservation of the old order and protection against chaos" (Covington 243). The idea of the heroine in classic literature isn't divorced from the idea of a hero. A woman is heroic if she defends patriarchal values and works to maintain the status quo, but she would be a nuisance or a villain if she were to work outside of that framework, or, God forbid, were to challenge it. A hero gets to defend his people, where a heroine gets to defend patriarchy. This is exemplified in a particular tale, "The Handless Maiden", where, "the king wanders while the queen rests—it is this juxtaposition that epitomises the dynamic relation between hero and heroine" (Covington 246). The classic heroine either gets to be a defender of patriarchy or a lady in waiting, where she is still upholding ideals of the patriarchy. The heroine will always exist in relation to and in the sphere of the hero/man. I believe that these classical representations of the heroine, and the passive role of the heroine archetype, are why I couldn't divorce the idea of the missing man from the woman's narrative. Where men get to stand on their own, women are most always placed in relation to men.

Evaristo redefines the heroine role in her work. Evaristo's protagonists achieve everything that they put their minds to, fulfilling the role of the classic male hero. The heroine is classically thought to possess characteristics of, "passivity, receptivity, and renewal [which] have been regarded as intrinsically 'feminine' and therefore innate in women, while the active, penetrating qualities of the hero have been seen as intrinsically 'masculine' and therefore innate in men" (Covington 252). However, the protagonists we meet in *Girl, Woman, Other* do not fit so neatly into this box. The women are people first, the heroes of their own story, who also happen to be women. The radical feminist protagonists embrace their female identity and use their actions to broaden the scope of femininity. Our heroines aren't celebrated for upholding the patriarchy, but for navigating a world outside of it.

The female identity is not limited to roles of femininity. But seeing women taking on traditionally-considered male roles and traits was a surprise in an all-woman narrative. This is exemplified through Amma's sexual behavior: "she worked her way through many of the women of Freedomia/ she wanted one-night stands, most wanted more than that/ it got to the point where she dreaded passing her former conquests in the corridors"(Evaristo 22). Amma views her partners as conquests and objectifies the women whom she sleeps with. This seems in conflict with her feminist disposition. In addition, Nzinga can be seen as fulfilling a male role through her control of Dominque: "why did Nzinga think being in love with her meant she had to give up her independence and submit completely? Wasn't that being like a male chauvinist" (Evaristo 92). Nzinga, who more clearly embodies a male-like role, is the villain in the first part of *Girl, Woman, Other*. She could possess these male traits to elevate her antagonistic status. Or, gender roles might just be much more complicated. The "politics of the body," a feminist critique of the 1960s and 1970s posits:

> An oppressor/oppressed model which theorizes men as possessing and wielding power over women—who are viewed correspondingly as themselves utterly powerless. This binary structure situates men as active, women as passive; men as violent, women as having violence done to them. (Brown 53)

Perhaps, placing women in male roles acts as a strategy to legitimize them as protagonists against patriarchal standards. A protagonist must be strong, men are strong, and so a strong woman protagonist must be like a man. I think that this is a compelling theory because we only really see the women from the opening of the book possessing these traits. Evaristo only has the first few narratives to make woman into hero, and convince those who subscribe to patriarchy that her protagonists are worth their salt. And in the first place, how much of our makeup is actually tied to our gender? Philosopher and Gender theorist Judith Butlers says that, "gendered identities are not a reflection of one's authentic core self but are a culturally coded effect of performance. Gender does not prescribe our performance; rather, it is a performance that ascribes our gender" (Brown 53). And perhaps *that* is the point that Evaristo is trying to make, that how we conduct ourselves is not gendered, or tied to gender. That "male" characteristics aren't limited to males, and that femininity exists outside of the binary.

Now to examine how Evaristo characterizes her men. In the narratives where they aren't absent (due to death, or abandoning the family), they are often posed as the villains. Take Trey for example, a man who rapes two of Evaristo's protagonists. Carole describes her experience: "then her body wasn't her own no more it belonged to them" (Evaristo 117). Two chapters later, LaTisha recalls her experience at the hands of Trey: "she wasn't expecting it and he was really pumping hard and making her sore and she struggled to move out from under what felt like a block of concrete and I don't want to, not yet, get off me, please, Trey, she said out loud to deaf ears so she gave up couldn't stop him"(Evaristo 194). Not only is he a bad actor, but he dehumanizes the women. Through their recollection of their experiences, Trey is seen as vile and completely irredeemable.

In contrast to the undeniable villain, let's look at a more complex male character. LaTisha's father left her family, leaving her mother alone to raise two girls, and leaving the family devastated at his departure. After spending her narrative condemning him for the state he left her family in, he returns and is accepted once again by the family unit. LaTisha chooses to accept him when she sees her son, "Jordan beamed up at his grandfather, with such an angelic look on his face/ she realized her youngest son needed her father in his life" (Evaristo 198). LaTisha feels that the absent father can't be replaced. Even though she, her sister, and her mother have been raising the children, that is no substitute for the real thing in the eyes of someone who places the value of the father above all else. While other family units, such as Carole and Bummi or Amma and Yazz, have existed and succeeded largely without the support of a father, LaTisha does not see her own family unit as a success and so she yearns to have the empty father role filled. However, her father is *still* the villain in this scenario. The reader cannot accept her father returning to the home, and wishes for the family to move on without him. We do not see him as a helpful addition to the family, rather as a force that undermines what the family already has. Even if LaTisha does not place him in the villain role in her narrative, his actions make him a villian to the audience.

And so, how *do* the women fair without the men? They are fantastic! They are much better off! Amma only ever needed a man to impregnate her, and has had a successful theater career characterized by feminism and lesbianism. Bummi started her own business as a single, immigrant mother. And she did this by herself, although she slept with her pastor to get the money to start her business. However, this is sort of seen as a power move, as "he behaved as if it was his right to pester his female parishioners, in which case, it was her right to ask him to loan her the money to start her business" (Evaristo 162). In this case, we view the pastor's actions as demoralizing, rather than crucifying Bummi for her proposition. And, we see Morgan become a social-media-famous trans activist, after leaving home and supporting themselves, with only their girlfriend and grandmother in their corner. Evaristo celebrates her heroines as they triumph over the patriarchy. She places the men in the story as obstacles and antagonistic forces to further elevate her women as heroes.

The men in Bernadine Evaristo's *Girl, Woman, Other* serve as the antithesis to woman. She writes the men as the bad actors, the antagonists, the villains. This is in direct juxtaposition to the heroism and accomplishments of the women. In classic literature, the woman's passive character is compared against the active character of man, legitimizing him as the good actor, the protagonist, the hero. Rather, here, the woman's character is compared against the man's to legitimize her independence and accomplishments in the face of adversity brought upon by the patriarchy. Evaristo places man as an obstacle to overcome, and an undermining force in the women's narrative. Heroines can only truly be heroic for women when they challenge patriarchy, or succeed in spite of it.

Works Cited

Brown, Jeffrey A. "Gender and the Action Heroine: Hardbodies and the 'Point of No Return.'" *Cinema Journal,* vol. 35, no. 3, 1996, pp. 52–71., https://doi.org/10.2307/1225765.

Covington, Coline. "In Search of the Heroine." *Journal of Analytical Psychology*, vol. 34, 1989, pp. 243–254.

Evaristo, Bernardine. *Girl, Woman, Other*. Penguin Books, 2019, https://booksvooks.com/nonscrolablepdf/girl-woman-other-pdf-bernardine-evaristo-2.html?page=3.

Faculty Writing

Introduction

Faculty writing reflects current, published work by Drexel University faculty. These texts have previously appeared in academic journals, conferences, magazines, newspapers, and websites. These examples of fiction, poetry, essays, and personal narratives serve to demonstrate all the wonderful forms that writing can take. Each piece is a product of these authors' experiences and expertise, and come together to form this poignant and thought-provoking collection.

—*The Editors*

Kathryn A. Dettmer
Translations: František Halas' "Whispered" and "Certitude"

On Translating František Halas

The poems here were chosen from the book *Krásné neštěstí (Beautiful Bad Luck* or *Unhappiness,* depending on how you read it), which was first published in 2006 by one of Halas's sons, a well-known radio presenter in the Czech Republic. The poems were published for the first time alongside the letters that Halas sent them in, to his wife, between the years 1928 and 1939. None of her correspondence is included in the volume.

I chose both poems because they delighted and challenged me. The first thing I discovered is that making things rhyme in Czech is much easier than in English. I was only able to preserve the rhyme in "Whispered," but since Halas was often accused of not being poetic enough, I figured he would not mind.

"Whispered"

A thin stalk is your body

from which grain fell without sprouting

how like a thin stalk is your body

A skein of silk is your body

desire written on the tissue's every last wrinkling

how like a skein of silk is your body

A burning sky is your body

furtively, a banshee with it, in the weaving

how like a burning sky is your body

The quiet is your body

its cry sets my eyelids trembling

how like the quiet is your body

"Certitude"

I enter into love and while blinded

feel my way, stumbling into the dark past

of your stricken mercies

I ransack and, unexpectedly and already, I know

it is not a given for me to stay in this paradise

I have so longed and yet do not belong

I pass though I renounce nothing

while staring into your noble eyes

there, I steal into half death half shadow

Tim Fitts
Flies

While driving my kids home from school, the subject of heartbreak arose. My oldest daughter had been dumped by her boyfriend. We were half a mile up Chapel Road from the school. Frankly, the conversation came as a welcome break. That morning, I had taken a shower, and water must have gotten behind my eardrum, because ever since, it felt like something bulging from the inside, and with every step, the sound of a balloon being tapped inside my head. However, as the day went by, the sound began to happen on its own, building from regular to erratic beats. In my mind, the seriousness of this ranged from inconsequential to grave. It was nice to have a divergent train of thought.

"So?" I said to my daughter.

"So, it *hurts*."

"It hurts who?"

"*Me*."

"On a scale of one to ten, how much does it hurt? To set a baseline, let's say a broken arm is five."

"A broken arm is five."

"Four or five, sure."

"A broken arm is not five."

"What is it then?"

"Nine."

"No way," I said. "First, you've never broken your arm. If you had, you'd know it's not that bad. Now, a compound fracture is a completely different thing. When the bone sticks out of your body, then nine is on the table. Do you know why?"

"No, Dad."

"Because it's not about the pain anymore. A compound fracture is about the fear. It's about seeing the bone in your arm when you're never supposed to see the bone in your arm. If you are looking at a bone sticking out of your arm, you have every reason to believe that you could lose that arm. You could suffer a bone infection and die within a couple days. You could die of shock. You could die of flipping fright."

"You can't die of fright."

"Shit," I said. "This is the problem with sixth graders. You get straight A's, but none of you have any real idea of what you're talking about. You can certainly die of fright! You can die of fright in the moment or even over the long run. It's probably the cause of every death, basically."

"That's comforting."

"Hey, that's life, pal. Let me ask you this. How much does this heartbreak hurt? Same thing. Scale from one to ten."

"*Nine.*"

As I turned to look at her, I felt a clump of wax fall from my ear, the ear in question. I had hoped that this had signaled some relief in the pressure, but no change in the erratic drumbeats. Maybe there was more to come.

"No way," I told her. "No way does this heartbreak hurt nine."

"How do you know?"

"Because I know. Same thing as the broken arm. You've got no house to split up, no finances to rummage through. No kids to share. Maybe this guy, this fellow has a new girl and has put a picture of them holding hands already on Facebook, or whatever, and has announced his new relationship to everybody. Which, if he has, I'll grant you two more points. Three maybe. Bonus pain. Has he done this?"

"Nobody uses Facebook anymore."

"Yes, they do."

"Yeah, old people who fight each other about politics and vote *dictators* into office."

"What do *young* people use then?"

"They use other things."

"Other things that are going to turn into the same thing."

"No, it won't. People in my generation aren't racists."

"So, I'll give you three. Three points for pain."

"Can I skip school tomorrow?"

I turned on the radio and let her take over the dial. My problem was that I had engaged. If she was going to suffer, she was going to suffer. We drove a few more blocks, and I told her that I was sorry. If it's nine, it's nine. She'll look back and see that it was three after all, but no sense pressing the issue.

The next morning, I awoke, and it was still dark outside. I thought it was happening again, except it felt as if one clump of earwax fell after another. Tumbling, almost. Instead of falling out, though, the clumps were crawling out. In the next moment, I realized it was not wax at all falling from my ear canal, but three flies had crawled out of my earhole. My stomach cooled. Of course, all I could think about was the legion of eggs inside embedded in all of that funk, what with their siblings and ancestry creeping about the gears and drum heads, all of the crannies, and either the good these maggots were doing or the havoc they were wreaking on my flesh. The sun had yet to come up, and when I pressed my fingers against my ears, I could hear the thrumming of wings reverberating inside the space they had found for themselves. All I knew is they were trying to find their way out, but until then, they were laying eggs of their own. Jesus, I thought. How long has this been going on?

Jordan M. Hyatt
(Co-author: Synøve Nygaard Andersen)

A Pennsylvania Prison Gets a Scandinavian-Style Makeover—and Shows How the U.S. Penal System Could Become More Humane

The United States has the largest number of people incarcerated in the world—about 25% of all people imprisoned worldwide are in American prisons and jails.

Overcrowding, violence and long sentences are common in U.S. prisons, often creating a climate of hopelessness for incarcerated people, as well as people who work there.

Additionally, correctional officers, often challenged by long shifts, worries about their own safety and stressful working conditions, have a life expectancy that is on average a decade less than the general population.

Some advocates have called for diverting people away from prisons, especially low-risk individuals. Others encourage shorter sentences and earlier releases.

But reform efforts could also extend to changing the prison environment itself.

We are American and Norwegian criminologists. While trying to better understand our countries' justice systems, we have spent significant time in correctional facilities across Scandinavia and the U.S. There, we often try to identify overlooked similarities within these very different places—and ways they could learn from each other.

A recent collaboration between correctional services in Pennsylvania and several Scandinavian countries presents an opportunity to test these ideas. One Pennsylvania prison unit we are researching adapts elements from Scandinavian prisons, and offers a window into what drawing from other penal systems might look like in the U.S.

Prisons in Scandinavia

Correctional systems throughout much of Scandinavia are guided by a general set of philosophical principles. In Sweden, these standards emphasize rehabilitation and encourage meaningful change, so incarcerated people can lead a better life.

In Norway, core values of safety, transparency and innovation are considered fundamental to the idea of creating normality in prison, the feeling that life as part of a community continues, even behind walls and bars.

Adhering to these principles means that, in some cases, incarcerated people can wear their own clothes, work in jobs that prepare them for employment and cook their own meals.

Prisons in Scandinavia are also small, with some housing roughly a dozen people—which is possible, given relatively low incarceration rates in the region.

In most cases, people in prison in Norway have access to many of the same social and educational services and programs as people who are not incarcerated.

Many prisons, especially in Norway, are designed in a fundamentally different way than in the U.S. Proximity to nature is often considered, for example. Cells in Norway are also for a single person—not multiple people, as in most cases in the U.S. Norway, perhaps unsurprisingly, has attracted many international visitors who come to observe their prison system.

Importantly, correctional officers have at least a two-year, university-level education and are directly involved in rehabilitation and planning for the incarcerated person's re-entry into the world outside of prison. In the U.S., most officers receive just a few weeks of training, and their work focuses mostly on maintaining safety and security.

It is also worth noting that recidivism rates in Scandinavia are low. In Norway, it has been reported that less than half of people released from prison are rearrested after three years. In Pennsylvania, that figure is closer to 70%. The implications for correctional systems are profound.

Norway and the U.S.

There are, of course, other fundamental differences between the Scandinavian countries and the U.S.

Norway, like the other countries in the region, is much smaller than the U.S., in both population and geography. Crime rates are lower there than in the U.S., and social support systems are more robust. Gun violence is also almost unheard of.

In Norway, the longest prison sentence in most cases is 21 years—with most people serving less than a year. In Pennsylvania, life sentences are not uncommon, and many crimes—including nonviolent ones—can result in decades of imprisonment.

Despite this, the two systems may not be completely incompatible, at least not when the goal is to reform the prison environment.

The Scandinavian Prison Project

In State Correctional Institution Chester, known as SCI Chester, a medium-security prison located just outside of Philadelphia, a correctional officer-guided team has worked since 2018 to incorporate Scandinavian penal principles into its own institution. Based on their direct experiences, the correctional officers and facility leaders sought to reconsider what incarceration could look like at SCI Chester. This initiative has uniquely focused on developing a single housing unit within the prison.

In 2019, the group, which also included outside researchers and correctional leaders, spent weeks visiting a range of facilities across Scandinavia, and the officers worked in Norwegian prisons alongside peer mentors.

In March 2020, six men in SCI Chester—each sentenced to life in prison—were selected to participate in the project as mentors. They then moved on to the new housing unit, which had come to be known as "Little Scandinavia."

In early 2022, the researchers and correctional leaders returned for a follow-up visit to several prisons in Sweden. Though delayed by the pandemic, 29 more residents of SCI Chester were selected from the prison's general population to join the Scandinavian-inspired housing unit that May.

With single cells, a communal kitchen, Nordic-like furnishings and a landscaped, outdoor green space, Little Scandinavia looks unlike any other U.S. prison. Plants grow throughout the common areas. A large fish tank, maintained by staff and residents, is the centerpiece of an area designed to encourage people to gather.

A grocery program allows all of the residents to purchase fresh foods—a rarity in prison—and work directly with staff to send orders to a local store. Each day, residents are expected to go to work, treatment or school, all within the prison. Importantly, the correctional officers overseeing Little Scandinavia have received a range of training to facilitate communication with their assigned residents.

Drawing from Norway's model, there is also a uniquely low ratio of trained staff to incarcerated men—one officer for eight residents, compared with the typical average of one staff member for 128 residents. Although the community is still evolving, there have been no acts of violence, as some speculated would happen—even with access to kitchen equipment.

Learning from Little Scandinavia

As part of our research, we are examining correctional staff's first-hand experiences with this international project.

Some analyses have shown that a Scandinavian approach, focused on normality and reintegration, can be potentially good for correctional officers, boosting their morale, independence and well-being.

Incarcerated people have also reported feeling safer and having more positive relationships with staff and other people living in the prisons. They also indicated greater satisfaction with their access to food and the reintegration support available to them.

SCI Chester shows that it is, in fact, possible to adapt Scandinavian-style penal philosophies and incorporate them into a Pennsylvania prison. This effort is a pilot, however, with significant costs, foundational support from committed leaders, and in partnership with many outside experts.

It remains to be seen how these efforts will play out in the long term. Data from this project, and rigorous research on other efforts, can inform conversations about what the future of prison reform in the U.S. could look like.

After all, as they say in Norway, a prison is responsible for enabling the people who are incarcerated to return to society as good neighbors—a fact that, in most cases, is as true in Philadelphia as it is in Stockholm or Oslo.

Henry Israeli
Coattails

i

I wanted to write a screenplay based on my father's life: from his birth in
poverty, how his family gathered around one scant meal a day of potatoes and
onions and maybe a knuckle of meat, to when the Russians came, teaching
them the glory of socialism and peasantry, and then the Germans who
rounded up the Jews of the town, separated men and women, and surrounded
them with machine guns, until the town madwoman cried out, *Run Jews!*
They're going to kill you, and my father and his father fled out of the square,
his mother and sisters gunned down in the dirt, and how my father and
grandfather survived two years hiding in a forest, nearly dying of hunger and
cold, until the Russians came again and drafted my grandfather into the Red
Army and soon after exiled him to death by starvation in a Siberian gulag, how
my father waited for him in Kyiv, taken in by the Jewish poet Hoffstein, how
when he heard of his father's death, fled the USSR and escaped to Switzerland
riding atop trains, then walked across the Alps into Italy where he embarked
on a ship bound for Palestine that was curtailed by the British who held him
in a refugee camp on the isle of Cyprus where he learned to be a lithograph
artist—and all of this before his eighteenth birthday, nearly the same age I was
when I presented my proposal.

ii

My stepmother looked me in the eye and said,

your father doesn't want you riding his coattails.

I turned to my father, his pupils beginning

to recede into the dullness of dementia.

He nodded in agreement although I knew he would

forget this ever happened in less than a minute.

Ride his coattails, I thought before crying myself

to sleep and dreaming I was swinging from the knotted tallit

of my father's prayer shawl as he belted out the *shemah,*

the final words on the lips of good Jews before sleep or death,

swaying there like a child on a swing no longer pushed

or a man dangling from the end of his rope.

Little did I know that one day my father would ride

my coattails as I carry him every day,

even now, more than twenty years

after his death, living out the endless echo

of a genocide that came so close to obliterating my birth,

my sisters' births, the birth of my daughter,

continuing the burden of the survivor, the one who made it,

the one who thinks he shouldn't have,

the one who tries so hard to keep the dead from dying

with words said in silent prayer bent over the page.

Miriam N. Kotzin
Rosie Married Down

Technician

Eldred heaved a broken rocker high onto the pile of scrap wood. He'd seeded the heaped pallets with rags soaked with fire-starter. He'd stay for the flames, for orange sparks riding air-currents skyward. The crowd would cheer his exploding fire. He walked away from the circle of light, night blind.

Plumage

Eldred and his friends were work fit, not gym fit. They wore plaid flannel shirts over plain tees like they'd never in all their lives gone to a concert or listened to music. Except for footgear, everything they wore looked soft from wear and washing. Eldred's ponytail skimmed his collar.

Rosie Married Down

"You'll live to regret it," her mother said, pumping lotion into a cupped palm. "In ten years you'll be me."

"I could do worse," Rosie said, picking up the lotion. "It's light," she said. "You're almost out." She set the bottle down without taking any. Fading bruises braceleted her wrist.

Mowing

Rosie liked mowing their lawn with the push mower with no motor—she'd bought it cheap at a yard sale. She said, "I can see where I been and where I got to go, and it's real plain what I missed. Nobody to thank or blame, anyway, but me."

Fashion

Rosie said her husband takes an interest in what she wears. He tells her what looks good on her and what she should take back to the Bon Ton shop. "Remember how I wore all that yellow? I loved yellow," Rosie said. "Now, anything yellow—stays right on the rack."

Smoke

When Eldred was 12, his cousin bought tobacco and papers and taught him to roll unfiltered cigs without a machine. He still smoked RYOs, a couple a day, some days carried one behind his right ear. Rosie kept the ashtrays clean. Every couple of weeks she smoked one he rolled.

A Companion

Rosie had breakfast conversations with the black cat wall clock. She liked to watch its big white eyes swivel and its tail swing. Regular as a pendulum, she talked, and the clock ticked. It kept good time and was good enough company. At supper, Eldred mostly would let her talk.

Motive

Rosie asked Eldridge why he'd married her. He said he didn't know. Then he shrugged, adding, "The only reason was I thought you wanted it."

If he'd wanted to make her happy, that was a pretty good start. She wondered how she'd spoiled it. The kit-cat clock rolled its eyes.

Baby, Baby

Rosie kitchy-kitchy-cooed toddlers in shopping carts. Sometimes Eldred grabbed her wrist, wrenching her away. Once she lost her balance and fell. He kept going, left the store, and drove away. She waited, repentant, near the checkout, until he pulled the car into the loading zone, windows down, radio blaring K-ROC.

To Save Money and the Planet

Eldred scowled and poked at the bowl of tomato-sauced spaghetti, dramatically lifting large forkfuls. "No Meatballs?"

Rosie explained Meatless Mondays.

The following Monday, Eldred set a bag of MacDonald's next to his dinner plate, unwrapped his two Big Macs and tucked in. Rosie promised that next Monday she'd make meatloaf.

Discovery

Eldred snored, but he couldn't help that. Day and night his chest rose and fell, his mouth open like a door left ajar. Rosie asked—and sometimes told— him to breathe through his nose, but she stopped short of telling him he looked stupid. How embarrassing—she'd married a mouth-breather.

Guilty Party

Rosie was always on him about something. She didn't like this, and she hated that. She couldn't stand it when he...anything. Even her kiss was a reproach. Eldred would've lost track of what was outlandish, or forbidden, except for her scolding him for his surpassing wickedness every blessed day.

Chilly

Rosie came into her mother's kitchen shivering. She hated heavy coats, and Eldred said she looked fat in her puffy jacket. Fat? Her mother shook her head and wound a red scarf around Rosie's neck. "Your Christmas present," she said. "But no sense waiting for Christmas when you're cold today."

Ally

If they were in the kitchen when Eldred called Rosie stupid, she'd look up at the kitty clock. She'd watch it roll its eyes, and she'd pretend kitty was mocking him. She had to be careful not to smile. He didn't like her to smile when he called her stupid.

Lifers

Eldred cracked his knuckles and said he'd "stepped into marriage sidewise—it fit no better than wet borrowed boots set to dry on a hot wood stove." He shook his head and said he'd like to dispatch Rosie. He'd trade connubial hard time for another life sentence in a heartbeat.

Flight

With the old-fashioned motorless push mower, the revolving blades whirring, Rosie could go any which way she pleased. She loved the sound the blades made. As long as she kept pushing, she could pretend she was one of a flock of mourning doves, all of them invisibly in flight, leaving.

Motive

Rosie asked Eldred why he'd married her. He said, "The only reason was I thought you wanted it."

She was quiet. I still do, she told herself and pressed her lips into a crimson line.

Eldred turned away from her silence and squinted, facing straight into the blinding afternoon sun.

Lynn Levin
The Silver Bullet

Frequent handwashing can help prevent the spread of COVID-19.
When I wasn't washing my hands, I remembered
when my normal germaphobia used to be called neurotic,
and I worried that my bandanna-and-rubber-band
face covering might fall off as I pushed my cart
through the grocery store. And what if I could not keep
from scratching the itch on my nose or if I
accidentally touched virused surfaces
after I'd pulled off my gloves? When I wasn't washing
my hands, I struggled to live with my adult children,
and they with me, hoping that we would come out of this
loving each other more, not less. When I wasn't
washing my hands, I reminisced about happy hour
with the girls: cocktails and half-priced appetizers,
wearing cologne and a nice blouse, going to work
for crying out loud. I watched a lot of TV news
when I wasn't washing my hands. In the midst
of the catastrophe, I cheered the clearing air
over Delhi, Seoul, Los Angeles, and New York.
I went for a hike. I was so happy to be outside
that I waved to strangers then saw by my footfalls
half-pint booze bottles, wads of fast food wrappers,
a dozen orange pill bottles, and three syringes.
I thought of laboratories, bats, ventilators,
and corpses shelved in refrigerated trailers,
the morgues and funeral parlors full,
and some of the poor laid to rest in mass graves.
When I wasn't washing my hands, I thought of
exhausted doctors and nurses toiling in the hospitals,
recalled Dr. Rieux and his helpers in *The Plague*,

Camus's great novel of resistance. I debated

which was better: to stay at home during the shutdown

or volunteer like those citizens handing out

bags of food to the suddenly unemployed?

When I was washing my hands, I drove

myself mad with the "Happy Birthday" song.

But that started to sound sarcastic, so I switched

to the "William Tell Overture," the theme of *The Lone Ranger*.

I saw the Masked Man and the wise Tonto

galloping in to stop the bad guys.

The Lone Ranger had a silver bullet and so did

Jenner, Pasteur, Ehrlich, Sabin, and Salk.

I wondered which masked researchers would ride

in to save us. I look for them now on the horizon

as they race against the clock.

Amanda McMillan Lequieu

"We Just Like It Here"—Identity and Community in a Wisconsin Former Mining Town

"When we first talked about getting married," Sheila admitted with a chuckle, "we thought he'd be in the mine, and we'd have it on easy street." She and Paul were high school sweethearts in the late 1950s, born and raised in the same northern Wisconsin village where, since 1880, their fathers and fathers' fathers had worked blue-collar jobs for middle-class wages in the deepest iron ore mine in the United States. When they got married in 1961, they lived in a city four hours from their childhood village while Sheila attended a two-year teachers' college. Sheila continued, "He's from Iron Belt also, so, we decided we didn't want to raise our children in the city and moved back." She groaned and shook her head. "And that's when the mine closed."

Without the smoke of the mills and the perpetual wages of multiple generations of industrial work, deindustrialized places seemed to lose their grip on their people.

In 1962, the founding industry of Iron County, Wisconsin collapsed. As changes in trade and technology abruptly ended mining, Iron County lost more than half of its blue-collar jobs. Like industrial communities across the Global North, Sheila and Paul's town, once central to the region's economic wellbeing, became a sucking vortex of economic depression. Within a decade, a third of Iron County's population packed up and sought their fortunes anywhere far away from the plummeting home values, public funding, infrastructure maintenance, and small businesses of Iron County.

Should They Stay or Should They Go?

Young, educated, and just starting life together, Sheila and Paul faced an important decision: should they stay in their deindustrialized home, or should they go? After all, the home they returned to looked very different to the one they had left a few years before. Home is more than just an idea; it takes place in the landscape and economy. For Sheila and Paul, the physical transformations of deindustrialization upended an imagined future of well-paid jobs settling them on easy street, surrounded by family and friends in the thriving community of their childhoods. Instead, they found themselves facing higher-than-average rates of poverty, joblessness and a very-place-based economic depression.

For the past 10 years, I've been puzzled by a question vital to social life in a constantly changing world: what is home in a place transformed by crisis? Core to what it means to be human, according to geographer Edward Relph, is "to live in a world that is filled with significant places: to be human is to have and know your place." It would follow, then, that crises that undermine the places people call home—climate change, political upheaval or economic crisis—would undermine a person's sense of home. And scholars of migration and disaster do consistently show how, in response to crisis, the dispersion of a place's people through forced or voluntary outmigration or the degradation of a physical place due to disaster causes domicide, or the death of home.

Transforming Ideas of Home

Community studies of deindustrialization in the American Midwest offer particularly pervasive examples of the transformation of both the landscapes and ideas of home. Through ethnographic research and interviews, I studied deindustrialization of a rural iron mining community and an urban manufacturing neighborhood because, between 1950 and 1990, between a quarter and half of residents fled communities that were quite literally constructed in the image of late 19th century industrial capital. Without the smoke of the mills, the creak of mine shaft elevators, and the perpetual wages of multiple generations of industrial work, deindustrialized places seemed to lose their grip on their people—and their place in the American story of progress.

And yet, in my study, I talked with more than 100 people like Sheila and Paul, for whom home never lost its grip. "I guess," Sheila mused with a smile. "we've lived here all of our lives." I raised my eyebrows and prompted them to explain why—and how—they stayed. They offered two answers that I heard again and again in other interviews. Counter to the dominant assumptions that crisis undermines home, people who lived through boom, bust and decades of aftermath described how their post-industrial communities offered them valuable material and ideological resources that would've been lost if they'd left.

On the one hand, remaining emplaced in the geographic site of home itself provided important material resources. Sheila and Paul's explanations for staying in Iron County in those first years after company closure emphasized how, through small choices, they made ends meet. With the lighthearted wonderment of those who barely dodged a significant disaster, the couple recounted how somehow, even in those hard, post-closure years, they prioritized the material benefits of staying in Iron County over hypothetically better economic fates elsewhere.

After losing his mining job, Paul turned to the familiar landscapes of his childhood and earned money working other natural resources—weather, woods and rock. Sheila remembered, "he drove a logging truck, and he also worked part-time for the town of Iron Belt in the winter plowing snow, in the summer, taking care of roads and stuff."

Staying near family meant that as the young couple started their family, they could lean on family members to help with caregiving when Sheila picked up work as a substitute teacher now and then. And plummeting home values in Iron County actually made homeownership more attainable for the newlyweds than they might have found in more economically stable areas.

Yet, stories of the pragmatic benefits of residential stability were only part of interviewee narratives of home. As life histories moved the narrative into more recent decades, interviewees shifted attention away from the residual material resources of a home in crisis, such as housing, employment or social supports, and towards the symbolic pleasures of remaining at home.

For Sheila and Paul, the weather was core to both their senses of home and ideas of self. The winters in northern Wisconsin begin early and often last until April, with cold winds from Lake Superior accumulating several hundred inches of snow over six months of frigid temperatures. Wrinkling her nose at the light flurries already falling from a blustery October sky, Sheila mused, "After the kids started moving, I thought, 'Oh good! Now we've got someplace to visit.' But it never entered our heads, even in the winter, to move somewhere else." Sheila smiled at her husband, deliberating a new direction to take this conversation.

"A lot of our friends now go to Florida or Arizona for the winter, three or four months. I don't know...We wouldn't even think of it," Paul interjected with the jutted chin of one who has resisted this suggestion on many occasions in the past. "I wouldn't mind going for, like, a few weeks," Sheila objected with a laugh. She continued, "We did travel extensively when we were younger— Europe, and islands, and Alaska. But to go anyplace for any length of time..." Her words faded and she joined her husband's resolutely shaking head. "I guess it's never entered our heads," she reflected honestly.

"We stick it out. We just like it around here." Paul agreed, softening. "I would never move; no, I would never leave here. Snow or more snow, I still won't leave." Sheila smiled and closed the subject with a brief summary, "It's just who we are."

When people call home a place that has transformed due to crisis and its long aftermath, their identities and material relationships reflect—and create—new meanings. Home is often marked by what Henri Lefebvre called "existential insideness"—a sense of ease and taken-for-grantedness embedded in a physical place, of "knowing implicitly that this place is where you belong."

Renegotiating The Meaning of Home

Deindustrialization threatened one version of existential insideness, but as people like Sheila and Paul stayed and strategized how to build a life in a hard economic context, they created new sources of identity, meaning and comfort. While easily making money is no longer possible in Iron County, making choices to stay in familiar landscapes marked by snowfall and deep social networks is. In fact, for all the griefs of iron and steel closures, the unknown territory of deindustrialization itself demanded residents' renegotiation and clarification of what place meant to them. Claims to meaning and identity are grounded in places that are meaningful both in spite of, and because of, being marked by deindustrialization. Here, without stability and within these constraints, home, both as a place and as an idea, is constantly being reshaped by people who stay. And again and again, interviewees' stories about their residential persistence centered on why, after decades of living in a crisis-riddled landscape, they want their home to remain here.

Just as home is not dead in Iron County, for many people, home remains in transforming places. Sociologists know this. The communities that motivate our research persist on islands that are quickly disappearing beneath rising waters, adjacent to hazardous waste sites, straddling fire lines, bridging tectonic plates, lodged between warring factions, or hidden within post-nuclear fallout zones.

Claims to meaning and identity are grounded in places that are meaningful both in spite of, and because of, being marked by deindustrialisation.

In these landscapes of crisis, residential persistence—and the quiet work being done by long-term residents—can be hard for onlookers to perceive. But home wracked by change or crisis is a sociologically important site of tension between the very real structural constraints embedded in place and the plasticity of choice and identity. Questions of "who we are" are intimately related to questions of "where we are."

References and further reading

Elliot, R. (2018). The Sociology of Climate Change as a Sociology of Loss. *European Journal of Sociology*, 59(3), 301–337. https://doi.org/10.1017/S0003975618000152.

Lefebvre, H. (1991). *The Production of Space*. Oxford: Blackwell.

Porteous, J. Douglas, & Sandra E. Smith. (2001). *Domicide: The Global Destruction Of Home*. Montreal and Kingston, CA: McGill-Queen's University Press.

Relph, E.C. (1976). *Place and Placelessness*. London: Pion.

Taylor, D. E. (2014). *Toxic Communities: Environmental Racism, Industrial Pollution, and Residential Mobility*. New York University Press.

Leah Mele
Her Body Lines

You should have stayed friends with her. You shouldn't have learned about her death through social media when your yoga teacher posted a picture of her smiling on the yoga mat, looking pale and dreamy as the sun hit her face. *Rest in peace.*

You made a beeline to the bathroom at work and hyperventilated in the corner stall. You didn't have permission to feel the way you did; you were the one who cut her out of your life. All of those friendships after her, you strived to find someone like her to get that close again. You had yet to match it.

Grief has a way of making things feel like yesterday. Memories that were inaccessible in the subconscious become unlocked and flood your mind. Suddenly, you were eighteen again when she took you to your first yoga class. She drove you to class in her tan Chevy Malibu that resembled a grandmother's car and trembled when the ignition turned on. She liked to drive with the sun visor down, not to protect her eyes from the glare, but she slid the mirror open to look at herself as she drove, finding her own vanity hilarious. You bent and flexed your bodies together and trembled in the poses.

She got better at yoga. Her body could withstand the demands of the poses and the heat. Her moves were untouchable, and she made everyone stare. You watched the yoga teacher give her more adjustments in class, and you craved the touch she received, or maybe you wanted her all to yourself.

You would give her a ride to the train station for her *Vinyasa* training. She'd wear leotards with high-waisted leggings and leg warmers into the city.

"On the train, I feel like Nina in *The Black Swan*," she said as she refreshed her makeup in your rearview mirror. "Remember that movie?"

You remembered. You'd watched the film *The Black Swan* together. She envied the ribs that protruded out of the ballerina's leotard, and you remember the throb radiating between your legs when Natalie Portman and Mila Kunis had sex. You didn't know you could get so turned on from watching women together. You wouldn't know that you were bisexual until much later.

Once, after a few drinks, she kissed you outside of a bar. Her long and devilish tongue hooked into the roof of your mouth. You grabbed her thick hair in your hands and pulled her close.

"Do you remember last night?" You whispered the next morning with your bodies interlocked on the single mattress in your parents' house. You could hear your blood pulse.

"Nothing," she had said as she rolled off the bed, out of your reach.

***

A psychic had warned you, after all. He had told you someone you loved would die in an accident. You were angry at the news. This psychic had broken a code. You were a trained clairvoyant, and you would never reveal such detrimental information during a reading. You only read the good things or harmless things like past lives and forcefully tuned out the bad. What good was it to tell someone that death was coming? Death was coming for all of us.

***

You ran into her mother at the grocery store.

"Do you still keep in touch?" she asked with an arm full of produce.

"No, unfortunately." We had a falling out. Her Chevy Malibu broke down, and she would come over to your house but then ask for a ride to her boyfriend's house. The habit kept reoccurring: each time she arrived, only for you to drop her off with disappointment. You eventually told her you couldn't do it anymore. You couldn't keep watching her leave. You wanted her to stay, and that's what ended things. But you never told her you loved her. You never knew if that would have changed anything or everything.

"She moved to Philly to teach yoga. She followed her dreams," her mother said with a proud smile.

Eventually, you moved into the city, too. You meant to go to her yoga class to reconnect, but you never did.

Now, you can't stop thinking about her body lines as she hung onto the man's back on his motorcycle. He didn't have an extra helmet for her, so her long black hair danced in the wet summer night. You wondered what the stars looked like that night when the storm rolled in after a dry summer day and made the streets wet and slippery. When the biker made a turn, she ejected into the sky. The lines her body made in the road when she landed, forever marking her end in asphalt unworthy of her perfection.

Keli B. O'Connor
Dans les Pas de Mon Père

Call it intuition, but I've been blessed with a precise sense of direction. Tell me your name and I've lost it just as quickly but drop me into a maze of streets and alleyways, and I will always find my way home. This, coupled with my sense of wonder, pointed me to a life of travel and adventure. I only wish someone had told my body this.

My muscles are wasting, slowly turning to fat. A summer ago, and after half a dozen misdiagnoses, I was diagnosed with a novel genetic disorder, a neuro-muscular degeneration so new it still doesn't have a name. Abilities I once took for granted, like walking modest distances and using a pen to write more than a page, have slowly been robbed from me. *C'est la vie.*

But it's hard to travel alone when the simple act of standing without tipping over is taxing. The cane helps, but canes prove all but useless without dexterity. My speckled pitbull-chow mix, Tofu, has been training to act as my counterbalance dog, a thankless task. She's tall and lean—statuesque, even—traits she inherited from her adoptive mother; however, she's strong and nimble. Her official job is to walk beside me as I used the handle of her vest to prevent me from falling. Her unofficial job is to be my best friend, so I won't feel so alone in a foreign country. We prepared for a French excursion for eight months, sitting, staying, maneuvering, and bracing. She was all set to help me navigate the winding, cobblestone streets of Collioure. Then, just before departure, a loosely tethered shepherd attacked her, leaving her with a piercing hole in her left tricep. After much deliberation, I decided to forge onward to a new, old-world alone, leaving her home with family and a protective cone to nurse her wounds.

I've traveled on my own before, but only to American cities. New York, New Orleans. Nothing old, especially not the old country. French blood courses through my veins, but only by way of my father's Canadian family.

It was appropriate that my first European experience would be at his paternal grandmother's home. Dad's where I got my love of exploration; he could never stay in one place for too long until his drinking bound him to his bed and, later, his grave. He can no longer explore the world, so now it's my job.

The plane from New York afforded me little sleep. A choir of babies sang a round to the overbooked cabin, but I was less than thrilled with the performance. For one, I think rounds are stupid, and two, I chose a redeye flight to catch some sleep before landing in a country where what little language I understand is cruelly butchered with a *Thpanish lithp.*

Somehow, with atrophied muscles and an intractable migraine, I landed in Spain unscathed, able to catch an afternoon train out to France.

As I hobbled on the platform in Barcelona, a blond, sun-kissed couple pushed past me, knocking my cane loose from the blistered tactile tile and into the side train beside me. The young couple, steeped in their mid-to-late-twenties, confidently sat in my seat on the 16:36 to Perpignan. An older woman, age sixty or a French seventy-five, approached them and said something in what was likely Catalan but could have easily been cursive. "Get out of my seat," she probably said, upsetting the pair. The young man puffed his chest and presented the lithe sage with their ticket.

"Ah, *mira*," she said, pointing to his ticket. "*Necessites el cotxe set, es sis.*"

The youths apologized, collected their overhead luggage, and forged their way through throngs of passengers to their correct seats. Before the woman could sit, I showed her my ticket and she granted me access to the window seat, where I hoped to get a peek of the Spanish countryside, and she sat beside me in seat 122.

From her bag, she squirted a dollop of hand sanitizer, but not the chemically clean scent Americans are accustomed to; no, hers smelled of fresh jasmine and the sea and handmade soap. European. The closest I've ever been to smelling that scent was from an expensive lotion sold in a tin tube at a strip mall "gift shoppe," the kind that sells Vera Bradley handbags beside those weird Willow Tree faceless mother-child figurines.

After thoroughly wringing her hands clean, she pulled a book from her tote—*Ma Vie Sur La Route—My Life of the Road,* the memoir of Gloria Steinem. My English copy, dog-eared and tattered, took permanent residence on my nightstand, but her copy, equally frayed, sat on the seat's tray table beside her phone. The screen lit up with a bouquet of colors, peace signs, and the time.

Her hair held clipped in a claw, not unlike mine, save for hers had the print of an old blue and white porcelain teacup, whereas mine was painted to look like a spotted dog. My spotted dog. Tofu would have loved it here.

My seatmate wore dangling feather earrings fashioned as butterflies in flight. The softest gauze pants I'd ever brushed up against, but maybe they were only so because of my captivation. She's all I think I ever want to be, at least in the life I'd imagined for her.

Her carefree lifestyle.

Her widowed love of travel.

Or maybe she never married. A spinster.

Unapologetically single.

Limitless.

Healthy.

From the intentional corner of my eye, I spy her fingering the pages of her book's first chapter, *Dans les pas de mon père. My Father's Footsteps.* I pried my eyes away from her and distracted myself with the fields of baled hay and rustic vineyards rushing past alternating sides of the tracks, but found my gaze wandering back to her. In the window reflections, I caught her swiveling her head, mimicking mine as if I was her guidepost to the interesting sights outside our train car windows. Then it struck me. Here I foolishly thought this was my story, but really it was hers. Perhaps one day, after jet-setting here or backpacking there, I'll reclaim it. Until then, I'll be busy shuffling around the world with my hair clipped back, wearing my softest gauzy pants, steady at my dog's side.

Don Riggs
Review of *Cascade*

Rosen's *Cascade* is the first book of a trilogy, *The Sleep of Reason*, alluding to Goya's etching of the same title, in which a young man is sleeping on his desk and swarms of bats, owls, and other denizens of the dark flock towards him—or is it from his dreaming brain? The titular Cascade refers to the major cataclysmic shift that has occurred an indefinite period before the novel's start, resulting in weird occurrences, like cracks appearing in the surface of the earth, people being transformed into demons, the sprouting of "shriekgrass" to replace edible crops, and the general appearance of magic. As one major character, a wizard, puts it, the question is not what can we do to preserve our way of life, but what does magic want?

Not all are infected by magic in their personal lives; a new category of human is the MAI, or Magic-Affected Individual. One of the most prominent of the MAI is Ian Mallory, an aging gay man initially from Newfoundland, who speaks with an accent apparently characteristic of that northern maritime province and is also used to persecution: "I grew up a skinny gay ginger in a fishing village in Newfoundland. I know how to take a fuckin' beating, okay?" For most of the early chapters of the novel, Mallory is hired as the court prognosticator for the Prime Minister of The Party, and as such is ultimately a target of The Opposition. This is in Canada, so I am not completely sure of the governmental structure, and when an individual is called a Senator, I must assume an equivalence to the US version, but with some doubt.

The *Cascade* cataclysm has apparently knocked the United States out of its position of power and dominance, although the SVAR—an acronym for the Silicon Valley Autonomous Region—has sent representatives to negotiate with the Canadian government. The novel constantly uses such acronyms for imaginary (in our world) organizations, and I had to underline them and note the page numbers for later reference. I would love to see a glossary in the next iteration of this novel, and its sequels. SVAR, MAI, the DRM (I still don't know what that one is), the magically amped-up NDA, etc. Mixed in with such acronyms are more conventional fantasy terms, like geas, which I assume fantasy readers will have no difficulty understanding (an obligation or prohibition magically imposed on someone).

There is a large community of characters that I had difficulty identifying at first, though the plot moved so quickly that I came to recognize the major characters ultimately—most of them before they died or were thrown out of power. Mallory has a distinctive edge to his character as well as vocabulary; his intern, Sujay Krishnamurthy, is another MAI who specializes in throwing a glamor—or is it glamour?—on people, which is why Mallory keeps her as a receptionist and assistant: she constantly keeps him in an appearance of health, looking rosier than his increasingly gray skin. She seems to be having a minor role for much of the novel, until it becomes apparent that the elder wizard has been mentoring her. She will undoubtedly play a much more major role in the second book.

One of the characters uses a bathysphere to go underwater and investigate the sudden appearance of a chasm; the vehicle presents an opportunity for naming: "officially...the *Nemo*" after Jules Verne's antisocial submarine commander, while the team "had christened it the *Love Craft*," which I naively thought was a reference to TV's *Love Boat*, but then I slapped my forehead: (H.P.) Lovecraft, of course!—and, in fact, they encounter an enormous Cthulhu-like monster, or the corpse of one, on their first expedition. Besides the driver and the team's leader, there is a young psychic girl whose function is to play an eerie melody on a plastic recorder: her "songs were simple, reed-thin and tinny, the broken cry of a dying loon....Woven through the melody was pain too deep to belong to a nine-year-old child." I'm not sure what function this live music plays in the bathysphere's operation, but this is one of the many "magitech" details that characterize this alternate post-cataclysmic Canada.

The fact that the novel was written by a Canadian and set in a future Canada has me, as a United States-born and-bred reader, constantly off-kilter. There are references that I have collected in my self-annotated copy. For example, "It was an orderly, very Canadian kind of apocalypse." I'm not sure exactly what this means, but I will accept it. Similarly, I will be sending this quote to a friend who lives in B.C. "There had been a semi-serious motion before City Council last year to give up on flood mitigation altogether and turn downtown Vancouver into the Venice of the North, navigated by gondolas and kayaks." How many of these references are in-jokes for those who know certain parts of Canada, or simply add detail and local color to the fantastic narrative?

The political wrangling between the two parties, one of which seems more accepting of magic and the other more inclined to prohibit it, is complicated by emotional and magical dimensions, influencing even form letters and resumé writing: "D'you think 'communion with eldritch powers' should go before or after 'proficiency with Microsoft Excel?'"However, by this part of the novel, where Sujay the intern is preparing for a job search after her party has been knocked from power, the reader has come to, if not identify, at least sympathize with the plights of the various characters, and feel a sense of unexpected relief when a character reappears after an evident demise. I am looking forward to, though not, like Ian Mallory, prognosticating about, the next volume.

Andrew Snover
Water Ice Was the First One

Here are the two things I can remember that together most starkly display the change. The second one was a plastic cooler piled full of striped bass, all dead. The first was when I was younger, maybe seven or eight years old. My parents had a houseguest in from the Netherlands, and we'd shown him the whole city. He played the bells on a Monday night, while the people sat around on picnic blankets and listened, and I ran around the grounds with a friend, chasing the lightning bugs.

After the recital my mother offered to take him out for dinner, but he said he had eaten too much that day, so he didn't need a whole meal. She came up with the idea of a soft pretzel and some water ice, to complete his tour of the city.

Water ice was a rare treat, and I finished mine eagerly. I watched the man pick at his medium Cherry and get about halfway through. The adult conversation swept on and he put the cup aside, and my mother asked, "Oh, don't you like the water ice?"

He answered politely in his accent, "Yes, but this too much for me." Then he handed it to my mother. She murmured an agreement that it did get too sweet after a little while. She dumped it out in the sink and threw the cup in the garbage.

And I, I ran from the room—furious at his ignorance and her nonchalance, ashamed to love something he could discard so easily. I couldn't tolerate that the gift had been wasted. So much wasted. It was one of the last times I can remember crying.

To get those striped bass, we first had to drink and waste everything. For someone's bachelor weekend we piled into many cars and drove the four hours down to the Eastern Shore and piled into a house and threw down our bags and then piled back out into the yard and drank. We finished around a dozen beers per man, a bottle of scotch passed around without a cap.

Most of the beer we drank during a game of bottle hockey. We felt quite liberated to be free of our women, and although the aim of the game is to make others quickly drink their beers, everyone was taking drinks even when their bottle had not been hit by the quarter. When there was a good shot, a general roar went up.

After the bottle hockey everyone was feeling nightish, even though the sun was still up. I fished all the leaves out of the pool with a net I found lying in the grass. I got the water clear of leaves but then we decided that for swimming the temperature was dropping too quickly. We had paid extra for a place with a pool, which now seemed a waste. Groups split off with a shrug, and some of us went out to the long dock to smoke cigars.

While we were at the end of the dock, someone mentioned Matt, who had died, and how good he'd been at bottle hockey. Someone said, "Such a shame."

And then a minute later he said, "Not the bottle hockey, I mean. Just the whole thing." Nobody spoke for a minute, as if we agreed to take a breath not just for Matt but for ourselves and for the time when we took to heart things like waste and loss.

Then soon we talked about high school, and the girls, and college and those girls. Jones bragged again and again about girls he'd gotten with. I finally told him that I had gotten with his favorite one, the one his wife still sometimes catches him texting. He asked me why I never told him before, and I said because I wanted to save it for just such an opportunity, when your mouth ran too much about her. And he said, "It didn't need to be a secret. I'm glad you did it. I wish we'd all fucked her." At first, I was put out that I'd saved the secret for so long to no great effect, but his reaction put me back in the spirit of fraternity and that was fitting.

There was a fire eventually, and we sat around it and looked out at the water and then into the flames. Bobby spoke about the war, but not in such a manner as to make us sad or angry. We could have been subdued by the wrong kind of story, but Bobby has an impressive touch with a story, and he navigated well. For some accomplishment on the ground, he won the privilege of going up with Navy pilots. It wasn't a trip anywhere—they just flew him around for a half hour and then landed back at the base. "Waste of gas, really," he laughed.

They told him beforehand that they would put him to sleep with the Gs. He didn't believe them, but they did it, even though he did the breathing. You're supposed to breathe like when women give birth, same thing. He did the breathing, but he said the edges of his vision narrowed in until he was looking at the world down a dark tunnel, and then he was out.

Guys eventually dropped off throughout the night, but I didn't notice until we were down to three or four. We were passing a cigar and another bottle of scotch and when I tried to guess the time, I said one, but it was three-thirty. Soon after that we went to sleep, because we had to be up for the fishing the next morning.

That's the only reason I mentioned the drinking, because of the fishing. The whole point of leaving Philadelphia was the fishing. It was a couple hundred dollars from each of us, and it didn't matter that we had no idea how to fish nor sail—we had been promised we wouldn't fail to catch something. We piled into cars and drove to a certain pier, and they loaded us onto a boat. We had a cooler full of beers and sodas and sandwiches, and a few guys even though it wasn't yet eight AM started with beers right away. I wanted to get my head under me before I started on beers.

It was a half hour run out into the main bay, and as soon as we slowed and floated for the first time the captain said that if he'd known how choppy it was he would have canceled, but since we were out anyway he'd let us catch some fish. It would be a waste to get all the way out there just to turn around. There was the captain and another man to hook and bait the lines, so all we had to do was feel for a bite and reel them in. They weren't biting at the first place we stopped to float.

He ran us another fifteen minutes out into the bay, and when we slowed down again a few guys started to vomit. They went off the back and vomited and tried to get some air, but nothing helped. The captain revved the motor for a minute to turn us into the swells and reduce how much we were pitching, but the waves kept working us around sideways.

Some guys jumped up to fish but morale was low. There was a picnic table on the deck and most of us were huddled onto it trying to master our stomachs. You could see on each man's face that his mind was focused inside, listening to his organs like an expectant mother when the baby kicks.

Another guy lost it and threw up, and then said he felt better. Then two minutes later he threw up again and said, "Don't do it; it doesn't help." He hung off the back for the rest of the trip, and people tried to help him but mostly to hope to keep it together everyone had to focus on themselves.

Someone caught a fish but it wasn't big enough to keep, and the captain motored us to the third location. There was another smaller boat there already, which was a good sign for fishing, but it was rolling so much that we got sick to look at it. We tried to keep our eyes on something steady, but there were only some low trees on the horizon. We didn't know how the captain picked the spots or found them. We would have been curious to know that, but we had to spend too much time on our stomachs. Conversations were a drain.

We went to another spot, or maybe we didn't. The day had begun to blur. We saw boats that must have been for pleasure, and others that must have been for work. I wondered whether they were having the same trouble we were, wasting their day.

The nausea sank in lower over time. We drank beers to feel better, and thought it worked, and then realized it didn't. At some point the fish began to bite.

We hauled them in and measured them and threw them into a cooler. Striped bass mostly. Beautiful fish. You wonder why they're called that, and then the sun catches them right and you see that they couldn't be called anything else. Each one came on deck to an incredulous cheer. We caught about twenty of them, for fifteen of us. Inside the cooler, the ones near the top would flop when you threw a new fish on them. I don't know if the ones on the bottom still flopped.

One guy on our trip was a chef. He's run a bunch of restaurants around Philadelphia. Places people have been. Anyway, he did a hell of a job with those fish. He had pork chops too, with the bone in, and steaks. There was a steak and a chop for everyone, and he grilled up three or four of the fish. We feasted, and I felt more seasick from the gluttony than I had from the boat. Or maybe the sickness just took a few hours to catch up.

We got ready to leave the next morning and there were still seventeen or eighteen of the beautiful striped bass, lined up in the cooler like pieces of firewood or busheled wheat. They weren't flashing anymore—like some of their shine hadn't been just the sun hitting scaly iridescence but somehow came from within. Dead they were dull. It was too early to think about eating, and we had a long drive ahead of us, so nobody wanted them. No more ice for the cooler anyhow. The day before, when we went to give the captain a tip, he had said, "I would love to take a few of those fish off your hands." But two of the guys had already lugged the cooler back up the dock, groaning and struggling, and it had seemed too hard to call them back.

That morning while we packed up the cars, someone took them out to the end of the dock and dumped them into the bay. Or maybe nobody did that. I'm not sure. They might've just left the whole thing to rot and chalked up the cooler as a loss. I didn't check.

On the drive home someone said he wished he had something cold because it might help his head, and it made me think of cherry water ice. It would've been wonderful to have some. We drove past a spot as soon as we were back in the city, but nobody spoke up, and we didn't stop.

Scott Warnock
The Rating is the Hardest Part

Pardon my bad Tom Petty "pun," as I was going to be more direct with this title: "School ratings: F---ed data (as if you didn't know)."

Stories have been piling up recently that yet again illuminate the hopelessness of school rankings.

One of the most compelling is a Columbia University professor's finding that the data that plopped his own institution at the top of the *U.S. News* rankings pile were dubious. In short, a math professor, Michael Thaddeus, showed that Columbia "had provided fraudulent data to the magazine," and the magazine unranked it. Then, as Akil Bello, director of the advocacy group FairTest, wrote in October in *The Chronicle of Higher Education,* after Columbia provided only some updated data, the editors "assigned competitive set values." Bello says of what the editors did: "In other words, the magazine made up data to keep a popular university in its rankings."

In another snowballing story, numerous highly ranked law schools are withdrawing from their participation in the rankings.

The problem is fundamental: Once you think you're going to make any sense of rating or ranking schools, you're in the world of mirrors.

There are things I suppose you might measure with schools—or are there? I was going to start my list with an easy "number of teachers" metric and then paused, realizing even a seemingly straightforward stat like that might need exploration: Full-time or part-time? Tenure-track or not? How is teaching valued at the institution and how in fact is that measured? And then to think that data will turn into a useful value to a particular human being...geez, when you put it like that...

Sports are fun, and it's no wonder we're so obsessed with them in our fractured society. There is an objective, agreed upon (for the vast majority of cases) outcome. Elections are like that too. Someone wins. Someone loses. The outcome is clear and obvious.

But almost anything with even a shade more depth doesn't lend itself to the "clear and accepted." Look at the effort online dating systems have made to create match algorithms (to be clear: Not that I would know).

What's the best place to live? The best ice cream? Greatest rock band? (Alright, so that's Led Zeppelin. Sorry). These are fun listicles that provide hours (and hours) of harmless argument. How about your best friend? Your perfect soulmate? Things are circumstantial. Schools are multi-layered, complex entities like that.

In "The Rankings Farce," Reed College president Colin Diver powerfully decries this "rankocracy," saying "the entire structure rests on mostly unaudited, self-reported information of dubious reliability." Diver lists not just *U.S. News* but other publications' efforts to rank colleges and says, "Taken individually, most of the factors are plausibly relevant to an evaluation of colleges. But one can readily see that any process purporting to produce a single comprehensive ranking of best colleges rests on a very shaky foundation."

Diver outlines six problems with such systems, ranging from the selection of variables to the weighting of variables (as an example, *U.S. News*, he said, "decreed" that six-year graduation rates were worth "precisely" 17.6%) to the overall issue of having the "chutzpah" to claim that an arbitrary, ever-changing formula "can produce a single, all-purpose measure of institutional quality."

But here we are, almost 2023, and this is still the way many people talk about not just colleges but schools all the way down the line to kindergarten. "How do you unring the bell of the socially accepted rankings?" Bello said in another *Chronicle of Higher Education* article, "Do the 'U.S. News' Rankings Rely on Dubious Data?" "That's the biggest challenge right now—is that the 'These colleges are good' and 'These colleges are bad' has entered the ether of the higher-ed admissions landscape."

You're not picking a taco. You're not buying a potato peeler. You're not even buying a car. When it comes to selecting a school, you're making a complicated decision. Don't let anyone fool you otherwise.

Eric A. Zillmer

Why Music?

Music is one of the great mysteries of life.

Why do we dance to music?

Why do we give the gift of music? What are we giving?

Why does music evoke such strong emotions and memories?

And why is there music?

An entire species of humans plays and listens to music.

Most scholars agree, music is essential in experiencing human life and creativity.

In fact, half of all Nobel Prize winners report playing a musical instrument.

Everyone can appreciate music, no prerequisites necessary, but music is, impossible to define. Theodor Adorno suggested that *"We don't understand music...music understands us."*

Street Music, 2nd & Chestnut Street, Philadelphia (Eric Zillmer, 2023)

The Brain and Music

The brain is a mysteriously complicated but ultimately beautiful three-pound organ. The brain has evolved to play a significant role in the human body, not only in sustaining the life of its owner, but also in playing a Fender Stratocaster.

Everything psychological is simultaneously biological. But how does the brain process sound to experience music? Surprisingly, there is no specific music center in the brain. And remarkably, music is processed, imagined, and understood, everywhere in the brain.

So, it is a neuropsychological fact that when you play the guitar you use many different regions in your brain. It's busier than a traffic intersection at Rittenhouse Square. Neuropsychologically, *"Nothing Else Matters"*(Metallica).

Because emotions enhance memory processes and music evokes strong emotions, music is neurologically involved in forming memories. That is why we remember a melody, for example, even after many years. So, when we give the gift of music, we present an offering of memories and emotions.

The Neuropsychology of a Rock Concert

The ultimate concert venue is the human brain.

When it comes to playing and listening to music, our brains are all-in. Attending a concert and listening to music makes us focus on the moment, a key ingredient in happiness. During a rock show we don't reflect on our regrets of the past or the anxieties of an uncertain future. Rock concerts celebrate the here and now!

When the brain processes music, the motor cortex in the brain is simultaneously activated. It is biologically natural to tap your foot, to move, and to dance. The concert music culture includes this tradition of expressing yourself through movement to music.

Music also has many therapeutic properties and has been used for the treatment of mental health issues, which was first pioneered by the Philadelphian Benjamin Rush, the Father of American Psychiatry.

Yes, attending a concert with your friends is and feels good.

The Electric Guitar

"The only time I'm happy is when I play my guitar." N.S.U. —Cream. The guitar is the coolest and most popular instrument in the world. You can pick one up for as little as $100...and it is portable.

And left-handers are invited. Five percent of all Martin Guitars are produced for left-handers. Zero percent of Steinway pianos are made for left-handers.

The guitar sound is unique, it is the attack and the sustain of the reverberation that makes it special, which can then be modified endlessly with different settings for pick-ups, amps, guitar pedals, and styles of playing.

EEG brain wave studies found that guitar players synchronize neurologically as well as musically when they jam together. The band Cream is known for their extended jam sets. Off the stage their personalities clashed, but in the studio their brains worked together well.

Playing the guitar has specific cognitive and emotional features that set it apart. It requires a high degree of sequencing, multi-tasking, planning, synchronization, motor speed, as well as neuro-emotional modulation. Therefore, learning the guitar can be difficult. It helps that the brain has mirror neurons, a certain type of brain cell involved in learning a skill by watching others, which is the easiest way to pick up playing the guitar, whether from a friend, a teacher, or YouTube.

Rhythms

Mozart suggested that *"music is not in the notes, but in the silence between."* Amadeus probably got it right. Two notes create a space-time continuum between them, which can be referred to as the basis of rhythm, a systematic pattern of musical sounds. Is it possible that the rhythm itself and not the melody defines the DNA of rock music? Absolutely, there is no melody without rhythm!

Much of our lives are immersed in different biological rhythms; our heartbeats, the circadian sleep-wake cycle, even seasons. And, not surprisingly, our brain wave patterns are organized in rhythms. Neurons typically fire in a rhythmic or synchronous pattern all associated with different levels of consciousness ranging from alert to asleep.

Neurons also fire in a consistent rhythmic pattern in response to collective behavior, such as a large group of people clapping or dancing to music at a Tower Theater concert. This neurological event creates a deep sense of team bonding among concert goers, but rhythmic music is also used at sporting events and even in military battle to form cohesion.

Different music genres have different rhythms, or beats-per-minute (BPM). EDM is typically at 128 BPM, but Spa music is close to zero BPM. Your choice of BPM for a music track can significantly alter your mood. Modulating the tempo is one of the easiest ways to change the mood of the music and the neurochemistry of your brain. Filmmakers know this and the soundtracks to movies have become an important artform.

What about the words and poetry used in rock music, do they include rhythm? Yes. Understanding speech and especially poetry conveys emotional intentions, through tone of voice, pitch, intensity, and rhythm. Thus, the lyrics of a song correspond to the verbal-sequential processing typically associated with the left-brain hemisphere, and the rhythm of language to right brain hemisphere spatial-holistic processing. This can be easily seen in the genre of rap music, which is almost exclusively words with a strong rhythmic beat, typically between 80 and 100 BPM, a groovy sweet spot for rap.

Why Music?

The fact is the brain has more neuronal mass dedicated to processing sounds than it does for words. Most scholars agree, music preceded language. Is music a language? Is language music? Is music more important than language? I would suggest, yes!

Music is principally made up of rhythms, which are linked to the anticipation of "what's next?" This ability to predict the future based on the timing and rhythm of events is a key ingredient in the evolution and survival of our species. From crossing Market Street, to showing up at our jobs on time, to knowing when to speak in a meeting, to hunting, building dwellings, and searching for a life-partner; it all involves a sequencing of events; rhythms. Our lives are like one extended drum solo. Timing and the anticipation of timing is everything. It is the soundtrack of our lives.

Ultimately, music is also very personal. Most humans who listen to or perform music are searching for something. Perhaps music is after all the key to creativity, our own personal journey, and just maybe, and the anticipation of what comes next, a realization of truth.

Sometimes, words and music come together in a beautiful weaving of rhythmic sounds and words, as they do with singer-songwriter Bob Dylan, who not only won 10 Grammy awards for his music, but also the 2016 Nobel Prize for literature.

"Don't Think Twice, It's All Right."

Contributors

Kiana Ahmari (she/her) is a Chemical Engineering Major who loves all things STEM and History. She has a passion for learning and educating. Her past writing experience includes co-writing the student-produced web series, *Stolen Powers*, and writing various papers for her classes. If she's not somewhere studying, you'll find her volunteering at the Penn Museum Archives.

Aviv Amdur is an interior design major who enjoys many creative activities such as writing, drawing, and dancing. She is an avid reader who loves to explore new worlds and experiences through the pages in her books.

Samya Bandukda is a Marketing and Business Analytics major at the Lebow College of Business. Outside of academics, she is deeply interested in exploring artistic outlets such as filmmaking and music composition. With over four years of writing experience, Samya is involved in creative writing newsletters and blog posts for a range of student organizations and initiated an international letter exchange program, "Beyond Borders," at her high school.

Matthew D'Esposito is currently a senior English major with a concentration in Literary Studies at Drexel University in Philadelphia, but his roots are in Brooklyn, New York. When not writing, he loves to watch movies, read (of course), complain about people his own age, try different types of hummus, and hang out with his friends. In the past, Matt has published work in the *Maya* literary magazine of which he is also the treasurer.

Kathryn A. Dettmer is an adjunct lecturer and instructor of French at the University of Pennsylvania and Drexel University. As a Peace Corps volunteer, she had the luck to learn Czech in a castle, located in the spa town of Poděbrady, before teaching English in an academic high school in Valašské Klobouky. She is currently translating the correspondence of an 18th century French botanist and erstwhile spy for the American Philosophical Society.

Keira Earley is an Environmental Science major from South Jersey. After graduation, she is interested in going into environmental consulting, and later, marine biology research. In her free time, Keira likes to read and make jewelry when she is not with friends. She also loves exploring the city of Philly and going to the Jersey shore over the summer.

Michael Emmert is a third-year English major with a Writing concentration at Drexel University. Previously he acted as a writer for *Write Now Philly*, publishing two articles on the site. In addition, he was an editing intern for Drexel Publishing Group, supporting the publication of the 2022 version of *The 33rd*. Michael enjoys writing about personal experience, utilizing both non-fiction and poetry to convey his stories. Outside of writing, he likes to paint and walk around the city of Philadelphia.

Chris Faunce is a senior studying Civil Engineering at Drexel. His poem "Staying Young" was written while taking Drexel's Writing Poetry course. His poems have been published in *The 33rd* and the Pennsylvania Poetry Society's *Prize Poems 2022* anthology.

Emily M. Fedon is a Chemical Engineering major graduating from Drexel in 2025. She is also minoring in writing and is in the Pennoni Honors College. Outside of classes, she is a member of WKDU (Drexel University's radio station), the fiber arts club, and the American Institute for Chemical Engineers.

Lillian Fenzil (she/her) has always loved storytelling, from having animated conversations with herself and others, to writing fictional short stories when she was young. To pursue this passion, she has completed the STAR Scholar program with a research project of exploring the process of writing a full-length novel, as well as engaging with Drexel's Writers Room on campus. She is a second-year Academic Counseling and Advising major in the Custom-Designed Program.

Grace Fisher is a third year double-major in English and Dance. She enjoys writing poetry, speculative fiction, and analysis of language, and literature. When not reading, writing, or dancing, she enjoys playing the piano and knitting, although not simultaneously. Grace recently completed her co-op working as a sports reporter in Dublin, Ireland.

Tim Fitts teaches in the Liberal Arts Department in the Curtis Institute of Music and the First-Year Writing Program at Drexel University. He is the author of three books of fiction and has published over fifty short stories.

Wren Francis (they/them) is a senior studying Criminology and Criminal Justice and minoring in Writing. They have been writing stories from a very young age, and have dreamed of becoming a published author for as long as they can remember. They love to bake but spend much of their free time working on the drafts of two different books, which they hope to be able to publish one day. They are incredibly honored to have been awarded a double win in this contest. They can't wait to see where else writing takes them!

Kathleen R. Grillo is a recent graduate of the College of Arts and Sciences with a degree in Chemistry and a minor in English. She loves anything to do with reading and writing and has a personal collection of over 300 books. She has written over fifty academic essays spanning an array of topics, including culture, STEM, and literature, three of which have been formally published.

Victoria Harrigan (she/her) is a rising Pre-Junior studying English with a concentration in Writing who recently finished her first Co-op with Drexel Publishing Group (DPG) as their Editing/Publishing Assistant. She is a competitive snowboard freestyler for Drexel's Ski and Snowboard Team (DUST) as well as Co-Chief Sports Editor for *The Triangle*, Drexel's independently student-run newspaper. In her free time, she likes to cook, take pictures with her camera, and work on her sports journalism and photojournalism skills.

Jordan M. Hyatt (J.D./ Ph.D.) is an Associate Professor in the Department of Criminology and Justice Studies and the Director of the Center for Public Policy, Drexel University.

Henry Israeli's most recent poetry collections are *Our Age of Anxiety* (White Pine Poetry Prize: 2019), and *god's breath hovering across the waters*, (Four Way Books: 2016), and as editor, *Lords of Misrule: 20 Years of Saturnalia Books* (Saturnalia: 2022). He is also the translator of three critically acclaimed books by Albanian poet Luljeta Lleshanaku. His poetry has appeared in numerous journals including *American Poetry Review, Boston Review, Plume, and The Harvard Review*, as well as several anthologies. He is also the founder and editor of Saturnalia Books and teaches in the English & Philosophy Department of Drexel University where he runs the annual Drexel Writing Festival and the Jewish Studies program.

Megan Kline is a first-year undergraduate student majoring in Marketing at Drexel University. She views marketing as a way to place her artistic expressions into the daily lives of others, contributing to her love of art. She enjoys working with creative mediums such as acrylic, oil paints, charcoal, and graphite. Despite writing never being her favorite, she still views it as creating art, but with her words.

Olivia Knestaut is a User Experience & Interaction Design Student from Wilmington, Delaware. She began exploring photography in high school when she received a Nikon DSLR as a present. Now she brings her camera everywhere to capture the world through her own eyes. While most of her time is spent in the digital world designing, coding, and photographing, she is a nature lover at heart and cares for a collection of wonderful plants.

Miriam N. Kotzin writes fiction and poetry. Her novel, *Right This Way*, was published by Spuyten Duyvil Press in 2023. It joins *Country Music* (Spuyten Duyvil Press 2017), a novel, *The Real Deal* (Brick House Press 2012), and a collection of flash fiction. She is the author of five collections of poetry, most recently, *Debris Field* (David Robert Books 2017). Her fiction and poetry have been published in a number of anthologies and publications such as *Shenandoah, Boulevard, Eclectica, Goliad Review, Mezzo Cammin, Offcourse, and Valparaiso Poetry Review*. Her micros have been published in or are forthcoming in *Blink Ink, 50-Word Stories, and Five Minutes*. She teaches creative writing and literature.

Annette Kroes is currently an Environmental Studies and Sustainability major at Drexel University. She is a big fan of science and art, and an avid writer from early in life. Though she enjoys creative writing the most, she has recently fallen in love with writing about science and the world. In addition to writing, Annette loves crocheting, watching mockumentaries, reading, and spending time with the people she loves.

Lynn Levin is Adjunct Associate Professor of English at Drexel University. Her debut collection of short stories *House Parties* was published by Spuyten Duyvil in 2023. She is also the author of the poetry collections *The Minor Virtues* (2020) and *Miss Plastique* (2013), both published by Ragged Sky.

Amanda McMillan Lequieu is an environmental sociologist and Assistant Professor in Sociology at Drexel University in Philadelphia, Pennsylvania. She earned her Ph.D. at the University of Wisconsin-Madison. Her research focuses on culture, social change, and home in the face of transforming economies and environments. Her book, *Who we are is where we are: Making home in the American Rust Belt*, is forthcoming with Columbia University Press in 2023.

Leah Mele-Bazaz is the author of *Laila: Held for a moment*. Excerpts from her memoir were shortlisted for the Eunice Williams Nonfiction Prize and a finalist for *The Southampton Review* Nonfiction Prize. Her writing appeared in *Schuylkill Valley Journal Online, Barren Magazine*, and elsewhere. In 2021, she won Barren Magazine's December Instagram Poetry Contest. She earned her MFA in Creative Writing at Drexel University, where she also teaches rhetoric and composition.

Elaria Mousa was born and raised in New Jersey. She is majoring in Health Sciences with plans to attend PA school. In her free time, she likes to cook, work out, and spend time with family.

Keli B. O'Connor is a novelist and First-Year Writing Program instructor at Drexel University. When she doesn't have a migraine, she enjoys nature hikes and petting dogs. When she does have one, she enjoys wearing stretchy pants while watching *House Hunters International* and petting dogs.

Julian Pittaoulis is a funny yet intelligent young man who can write great personal narratives and stories. He has prior experience as a secretary writer for the National Junior Honors Society at his middle school in Philadelphia as well as being an article editor for the *Centralizer* newspaper at Central High. He is currently a freshman studying Business and Economics at Drexel's Lebow College. He enjoys making and producing music, songwriting, going to the gym, and playing soccer.

Don Riggs has been reading science fiction since fifth grade and has been teaching that genre for about a quarter century. He loves writing reviews of new science fiction novels and anthologies because they keep him aware of what is currently happening in the field.

Andrew Snover recently earned his MFA in Creative Writing from Drexel. His work has appeared or is forthcoming in *Streetlight Magazine* and the *Tusculum Review*. He is currently revising his second novel manuscript, and querying agents on his first. He can usually be found reading aloud to his children or watching the 76ers on an iPad while doing the dishes.

Sharon Sohmen is a first-year Computer Engineering major. She started writing in the 4th grade, when she won an alumni-sponsored writing competition at her elementary school. She was later chosen to read her essay during her upper elementary "graduation." Most recently, she won a senior award from her high school's English department and a scholarship prize for an essay she wrote. For her, writing has been a meaningful way to express her gratitude for the people and institutions in her life, and she hopes that in whichever way writing will be a part of her future, it will honor those who have made her who she is.

Cassandra Stathis was born and raised in New Jersey but spent a lot of their weekends in the city of Philadelphia, where they decided to go for college to major in English and minor in Psychology. Before coming to Drexel, Cas had ten articles published for Rider's University school newspaper, *The Rider News*. In their free time, Cas likes to collect comic books and create cosplays for Dungeons & Dragons characters.

Melissa Stellenwerf is a striving Interior Design student at Drexel University who is ready to make her mark on our rapidly changing world. When she's not studying, she loves to experiment with all forms of art including painting, sketching, collage and sculpture. With her family close at heart and the environment in her mind, she is striving to create a more community-oriented and sustainable future.

Alexandra Talarico studies Biological Sciences and minors in Writing to better understand what life is and how life feels. She is an active member of the Reginato Lab at DUCOM, a child life volunteer at CHOP, and a mentor with the Science-Mentorship Institute where she encourages underrepresented high school students to pursue higher educations in STEM. Outside of the classroom, she is actively drafting the manuscript for her first novel. When she's not performing cell cultures or obnoxiously clicking away at her keyboard, you can find her curating niche Spotify playlists and justifying why another $7 iced latte is an investment in her future.

Brooke Thompson is a Biology major on a pre-med track and is set to graduate in June 2026. She enjoys running, reading, and art. This is one of the first pieces she has written here at Drexel but plans to continue writing and hopes to take some creative writing classes in the future.

TJ Ton is a first-year Computer Science major at Drexel University. In his free time, he likes to go out, explore, and gain as many new experiences as he can. He is an avid cat lover and has 5 cats. He has always enjoyed searching for beauty in everyday life and has only recently discovered the art that lies within writing. TJ is very grateful for the professors and mentors who have guided him to appreciate literature and taught him to give his all no matter what he is doing.

Justin Veloz is an undergraduate student at Drexel University currently majoring in Chemical Engineering with an interest in emerging technologies improving the way we live. Growing up in a Hispanic American household big into the culture of sports, Justin found himself developing an interest in combat sports such as boxing and mixed martial arts at a young age. Unable to turn off his curious mind, he found himself invested in, not just the rich culture and history behind combat sports, but also with the risks and limitations present.

Scott Warnock (Ph.D.) is a professor of English and Associate Dean of Undergraduate Education in the College of Arts and Sciences at Drexel. He teaches a variety of courses and is widely published in the areas of online writing instruction, computers and composition, and education technology. Warnock has served as an officer in several professional organizations, including as president of the Global Society of Online Literacy Educators. He is president of the Palmyra High School Foundation for Educational Excellence and has coached youth sports in his community since 2005. He writes the blog/column "Virtual Children" for the Website *When Falls the Coliseum*.

Randee Wismer is an English major with a literary studies concentration in the graduating class of 2023. She has been published previously in the Drexel Publishing Group's online magazine, *Write Now Philly*, and in Drexel's undergraduate literary magazine, *Maya*. She enjoys writing, hanging out, and laughing.

Conway Zheng is a second year Materials Science and Engineering student. He is ambitious in getting involved with the materials field and did research over the summer of his freshman year with Drexel's STAR Scholars program. His hobbies include drawing and crocheting. Conway doesn't consider himself to be very good at writing and likes STEM classes more than English classes. However, with the encouragement and help of Dr. Nulton, he was willing to embrace English writing for a try.

Eric A. Zillmer is the Carl R. Pacifico Professor of Neuropsychology in the Department of Psychological and Brain Sciences at Drexel University in Philadelphia, where he teaches a course on the Psychology of Music. He is the author of the textbook *Principles of Neuropsychology*, as well as an accomplished musician and the President of the Philadelphia Classical Guitar Society.